LOOKING THROUGH THE LENS

SCIENTIFIC ENRICHMENT OF OUR CHILDREN

Dr. Martin Roy Edward

ISBN 979-8-89322-298-2

This book is dedicated to my wife

Mrs. Tejovathi Martin

and

my Loving daughter

Ms. Norika Martin Edward

Contents

Preface

This book titled **"Looking through the Lens: Scientific Enrichment of Our Children"** is mainly dealing with the methods of science education and the problems faced in the education of Science in our country. This is based on my observations and in-depth study of science teaching in the urban and the rural areas in our country. The sorriest part of the whole story is that most of the children on completion of their studies goes abroad and work there. Which I feel is a colossal loose of our revenue and our effort were our own children are not available for our nations growth.

I do have the feeling, that the teaching of science seems to be better in our country during the British Rule. I make this statement because we were able to produce some eminent scientist like Sir C. V. Raman, Dr. Homi Bhaba, Dr. Vikram Sarabhai, Dr. Birbal Sahani, Dr. Varghese Kurian, Dr. M.S. Swaminathan and so on. We were also able to produce two Noble prize laureates such as Sir C. V. Raman and Rabindranath Tagore who got the Noble prize when we were under the British Raj. After our country became independence and during the last seventy-five years we were not able to produce eminent scientist or get any Noble Prize for our country in the field of science and literature. Now the question is will we be able to regain the same glory once again. Well I am sure we could, provided we all get together and strive our best to achieve it.

A lot need to be done in the field of science education. As we all know that we are all living is an era of science and technology, and this has changed the style of our living. Even though we have brought large changes in our society, but the attitude of mankind has not changed. We have become more and more greedy and more selfish. Our undeterred use of the natural resources around the world is shrinking and it is becoming scarce. If we keep on depleting our natural resources in this manner, then our future generations will not be able to see or enjoy these resources. So, it is essential that we try to bring an attitudinal change in mankind, so we are able to conserve our natural resources for the future generations. This attitudinal change can be brought in only by educating the masses.

It is due to this reason why science education is very important for the development of any nation. We may have a glorious past in the development of science. However, a well-planned and a systematic science education for the masses was first brought in the country by the British. This legacy was continued with proper improvement in the system of science education after Independence by our first Prime Minister Late Shri Jawaharlal Nehru who had a vision and laid the foundations of science education and started several Scientific Research and development Institutes in our country.

Though we have achieved well in the field of science education soon after independence, and we had the highest number of science graduates and post graduates produced in the country. This resulted in the brain drain of the talented youth from our country to the developed countries such as the United States of America, Canada, and other European countries. The main reason was that the Indian Government didn't have sufficient infrastructure so that these talented and educated youths could be provided suitable employment opportunities.

Here I would like to state that there was a considerable fall in the research publications in our country, by the end of 1980's and it further declined by the end of 1990's. This was due to the undeterred interference of politics of this country in scientific development. There was shortage of infrastructure such as the engineering colleges then in the past and today we are facing the crisis of not having sufficient medical colleges in the country. We need sufficient doctors to take care of our large population in the country. It has been seen that most of our student's travel to countries such as China, Russia, Philippians for medical education and it has been seen that most of the children after completing their medical education, only a few come back to our country to render their services to this nation.

The most important factor that needs to be noted is that the number of students seeking admissions for basic sciences and for basic science research is also very down and more effort is put on for applied research. As per my opinion the basic science research is more important than the applied research, this is because without basic science research we cannot go for applied research. So lately we had to introduce institute for basic sciences research in our country.

During the year 1990 – 2000 the period of my teaching in Kendriya Vidyalaya, I have observed that the number of students opting for science stream declined considerably and most of the students opted for commerce and preferred to go for administrative services. It was my observation that even the most highly talented students also preferred to go for Administrative services and none of them showed much interest in getting into the science Education.

With the development of science and technology and now has its effects have reached the rural parts of our country, and with this effect, the science education in our country has gained momentum and now more and more students are attracted towards learning science. As we know that nearly seventy percent of our population lives in the rural areas and as the number of schools and colleges move towards the rural areas the boon for studying science has increased.

However, the teaching of science in the rural areas needs to still gain momentum. The rural science teacher should be trained properly and they need to be motivated so that they are able to train our students properly with the available resources in the rural areas. So that these children could come out and carry out R&D for the proper development of the rural areas.

One of the main characteristics of man, is that he is a keen observer and he is always curious to know more about his surroundings and the types of changes that is taking place around him. He is the only organism who has been provided the sense of thinking, and imagination. Man has developed his own method of knowing things and his own methods of enquiry to understand the wonders of nature that is occurring around him.

Science is dynamic, and it is an expanding body of knowledge which covers every aspect of new dimensions of human experiences. We also have developed a methodology which is adapted for seeking knowledge. This is called as scientific methods which involves several interconnected steps all of which finally arrive at the appropriate principles, theories and the laws that governs the physical world. It's important that we should bear in mind that the laws of science are never viewed to be the fixed eternal truth, this is because even the most established and the well-known universal laws of science are always regarded as the provisional and can be subjected to modifications in the light of new observation, experimentations and analysis.

Science is a social endeavor, science can be considered as a good and an evil master. This is because science is knowledge and knowledge is power, and with power comes wisdom and liberation, at the same time science can lead in breeding of arrogance, tyranny. Science do have the potential to be beneficial and harmful, emancipation or oppressive. In the twentieth century we have several examples which could speak about the dual role of science.

What should be the aim of science education in our country? Our science education should be closely related to the curriculum and it should be based on the policies that are developed for the development of human resources. It should also aim as an expression of the expectations from the education which includes the people's educational needs and their demands. Whenever we are planning for science education it is important that we mainly focus on the various roles the people plays in their near future. Therefore, it is essential that we plan our curriculum by keeping a foresight and a vision for the future of our country. Every effort should be made to see that our children on completion of the study should be able to develop confidence and be courageous that they would be able to excel well if they are provided with a proper placement on the completion of their studies.

As per the available statistics the average students access to science education in our country is nearly thirty percentages. Today as we all know that we are living in a globally competitive world. We should be aware of the fact, that we shall be able to excel well in any field only if we are able to compete successfully in this global era. This is only possible if we are able to train our children in science and technology in a better way, this is possible only when our children are properly educated and trained well to face the competitive world economy.

If we are able to consider the number of students admitted in our schools in the primary classes up to the secondary level. All those who are entering into our educational system do have full of vigor, zest, vitality and curiosity. Most of the children lose their interest in their studies. Our teachers in the primary and the secondary level is not able to maintain these children's vigor, zest, vitality and curiosity. The inborn talent of the child's quest of questioning the teacher about their doubts which is raised out of curiosity, would never been answered to the child by our teacher but the child will be scolded and made them to keep quiet. In fact, the child's desire and zest to know things is squashed, suppressed and crushed by our own teachers in the school.

As stated earlier, the teaching of science in the rural areas are not up to the mark, we need to put more effort for the improvement of science education in the rural areas. We need to have proper schools, well qualified teachers and there should be a proper regular inspection and regular follow up of the teachers teaching, this would tow up the proper functioning of the rural schools. Most of the state and the central Boards boost their results with the schools of the urban and the rural areas. If these boards are directed to declare the results separately for the urban and the rural schools, then the true situation of education in our country would come up.

This poor performance of rural schools in our country is due to the corrupt practices adopted by the rural level education officers in the state, who has the responsibility of regularly inspecting the rural schools and is also responsible for the improving the quality of education and improve the status of the rural schools in the country. If we need the status of the rural areas to improve in education, then these rural level education officers should be made accountable.

Our examination system needs to be improved the present day examination system has resulted into the development of several coaching classes in each and every city in our country. There are many coaching classes in those cities where the state or central boards are present and a lot of different types of malpractices are also seen. As a result, it has been seen that the students are put under physical and psychological stress. To keep a check on this situation it is necessary that we bring reforms in our examination system and the method of evaluation in Science.

A chapter on the teaching of science at the early childhood years has been introduced, this has been done so that the children right from the early years have been seen to perform such things which really astonishes the adults. Several studies have been done in the field of child developmental and cognitive psychology. These studies have proved that the environmental surroundings in which the child lives would effect a lot and that will have more importance during the early years of infancy and it is this decides and brings the required changes in the child and these do have a long lasting effect on the child's development. Several studies have also shown that if there is a lack of needed stimuli provided to the child, then this may result in the child's development without the child reaching up to their full potential. It is this reason why science education in the early childhood years do have greater importance in many aspects in the child's development. There are several reasons, why the science education should start right from the early years of schooling has been narrated in this book.

Curiosity is one of the inborn characteristics that is seen in all the children, and this characteristic needs to be properly nurtured, fostered and motivated by our teachers in the school. It has been seen in our schools that when the child questioning a teacher out of curiosity to get more information of nature or his surroundings then the question is never answered by the teacher instead the teacher scolds and threatens the child. I have seen this type of things happening in most of the Kendriya Vidyalaya's and more particularly in mathematics class. When the child asks some doubt in the class the teacher makes the child a laughing stock in the class so the child loses interest in the subject and due to this most of the children remain poor in that subject.

In short it is important that the child's curiosity is well maintained by the teacher throughout the child's study in the school. If we are able to maintain the child's curiosity in the school throughout then this will lead to a very good performance of our children in their education in the future and they would perform well in their higher education. All this depends upon the teachers how they manage with the students and I have experienced it during my years of teaching in KVS. A lot needs to be done for the improvement of teaching science in our country.

One of the most important factor which I have seen in most of the schools about the teaching of science is mostly examination oriented. I don't think that the examination system in our country is properly designed in a scientific manner. The examination system and the evaluation pattern process does not have any correlation between the teaching of science and its evaluation. It looks that the examination system in our country is mainly designed and framed to check the children's mechanical type of testing, it looks and I feel that our examination system is designed for the testing of our children's ability to memorize and reproduce the answers to the specific set of questions provided in the examination. It looks that our examination system is designed in such a way that we are able to prepare children who are capable of producing children who can reproduce answers mechanically just like robots that to for selective set of questions.

I have come across a case where the child has written the answers correctly in the test paper but the answer was scored off by the teacher saying the answer is not presented in the way it was given in the notes that was provided to the children in the class by the teacher. When I went through the child's test paper; then I found that the child's answer to be correct, the only thing which I found was the child has written the answer in her own words but the answer was correct but the teacher was not ready to accept the child's version of presenting the answer. But after the discussion the teacher has accepted his mistakes. Such things also do occur in the schools. Yes, I feel that the children should be encouraged to write the answers in their own words rather than following the bookish language or the language of the teacher provided in the notes. The child will be able to write the answer in their own words only when the child is clear with the subject and when the basics concepts are very clear. We should encourage such practices in the schools and the teachers should be trained to do so.

One of the greatest problem with our present generation of children is that they are not able to apply their own knowledge to any unknown situation and try to solve them. This is mainly because, the examining body the Educational Board, whether central or state boards comes out with the sample papers, guide books and other texts under various nomenclatures which is stated as guide materials or support materials for the coming board examination. A well experienced teacher will be able to predict the probable questions that would appear in the board examination, based on this there will be selective teaching and learning. Due to this type of learning the children are not able to retain what they have learned and they will easily forget what they have learned. This is mainly because the children are not trained through science by doing method. Therefore, the chance of children's retention of what they have been taught is very less. Hence, if we want that our children should excel in science and progress well in science throughout their life then we should be able to stop the production of these study material and guide books.

It is important to learn that the children do also plays an important role as an active agent; in their personal acquisition of knowledge. All the instructional approaches made would aim to promote active learning among the children, through the use of hands on activities which needs to be carried out in small groups and this would also help in a sense of making our children to think and discuss issues among themselves. It can also be expected that our children will be able to construct and develop a proper understanding of the scientific context of our environment around them in a proper way by using the inquiry based learning technique.

We need to have a very well planned and a properly guided inquiry based instructional approach for teaching science. This would allow and help our children in building the new concepts, and with this our children will be able to acquire the required knowledge with their existing mental model. This act will also help these children to utilize the same knowledge acquired to develop their own new activities. Where as in a guided inquiry approach, the children are expected to be an active member or an agent in the learning of various activities. This would really help the children to strengthen the children's sense of ownership of their own work and this would enhance the child's zeal and motivates them for the understanding of the new science concepts. If we have a systematically and properly planned approach with these children, then we should be working in small groups and this would help in promoting their collaborative skills and this will gradually provide opportunities for the children and help them to develop a proper peer understanding. The science activities that are formed should have relevance to the child's daily lives and this would allow the children to make connections between what they already know and what they are learning.

There are various conceptual methods that has been incorporated in this chapter such as the inquiry based learning and how it can be integrated with the text book based education. The teaching methods that can be used effectively. In this book the author narrates the importance of play and how this play helps the children to gain mastery on certain skills and they will also have control over their environment. The author has tried to express the importance of the environment and how the physical environment may vary depending upon the age of the child and the number of children present in the class room and how it would effect on the goals of the program that needs to be achieved. The word learning centers have been introduced. The learning centers are referred to learning areas were the learning really takes place in the class room.

Here in this book the author has tried to make an imaginative sketch of the ECCE class room along with the safety measures that is required in the ECCE class room, and has stressed the importance of play with the definition of the word play and its characteristics. The importance of play in the cognitive development of the child, the role of play in the social development of the child, emotional development of the play, development of language through play, the play also helps in the physical development creativity and other developmental benefits of play has been described.

A separate chapter has been introduced on the play way method of teaching children at the Preprimary and primary level. This was a method which came into existence with the work of an educator Fredrich Froebel. He was the man behind the development of Kindergarten concept. His main objective was to introduce the spirit of play in the educational institutions. He believed that the best way for the children to learn was through the medium of guided play in a friendly natural environment. In this chapter the author points out the effectiveness of the play way method of teaching. The principles of play way method of teaching, and why should we adopt the play way method of teaching at this stage of child's growth. He has tried to narrate the role of teachers in play way teaching along with the procedural details in play way method. I am confident that this would be a good book for reference for the teachers teaching the Preprimary and the primary classes.

A chapter on the pedagogy of teaching children at the foundational stage has been included, which would be describing the act of teaching. The pedagogy adopted by the teacher mainly shapes their actions, judgments, and the teaching strategies by taking into consideration of the theories of learning, understanding the students and their needs, their backgrounds and their interest of each and every individual student. Here the play is the center of learning and development at this stage. This play can be free, guided or structured, various activities such as conversations, stories, music, various types of movements, arts, craft, toys, and games are the part of play and these methods are to engage children in play where as other methods can be innovated. Once again it has been narrated that the planning is the main requisite for the class room teaching.

It is my observation that when the children are directed to prepare any science topic without any help of a teacher, or when they have to prepare a topic of their own, then it has been seen that the children do it in a better way by collecting the required information from various sources available and prepare them in a better way and present properly. It is also seen that the children would be well prepared even to face any questions posed by their teacher or anybody else. It has also been seen that the knowledge acquired by the child would be better then what they have acquired from their class room teaching from their teacher. It has also been seen that the children would be very clear about the basic scientific concepts of the topic and the child could master the topic in a better way, this type of the work performed by the children is called as learning by enquiry method which is carried out by the child, does have some important significance that has been narrated in this book.

This book mainly defines the term science of inquiry, the book also defines scientific methodology and makes an analysis of it. In a country were the teaching is mainly done on by using the traditional method such as the chalk and talk method. Under these conditions the use of the Inquiry based science Education would be quite difficult. This is because the teachers should be well equipped and prepared with the latest developments and shall be well informed and up to date in their subject by constantly reading and updating their knowledge. Then only the teachers would be able to use this method of teaching and guide the children in a proper way by using this inquiry based Science education.

This method of teaching has been proved as one of the best methodologies in the present days teaching of science, but the same cannot be implemented in our country. Even the teachers are also not ready to implement the same in the teaching learning process of science teaching at the school level and the reasons have been presented in this book. The author has given a detail account on this methodology in details which could be a good reading for all the teacher in the schools for understanding this methodology and implementing the same in their schools.

The teaching of science is usually done in the primary classes in the form of environmental sciences. The author has tried to throw light on the most controversial topic that is going on today. That is the evaluation process at the primary level. This process of evaluation that is going on in our schools and in higher educational institutions in our country brings a feeling of insecurity, stress, anxiety and humiliation to most of our children who are going to schools, but not only in schools but the students studying in higher education also faces the same problem. Hence, a lot of work needs to be done on this line of educational evaluation in our country.

Whenever, we are assessing a child then we should be always aware of certain facts about the child so that the teacher could adopt certain strategies to groom the child properly and how the child could be assessed during the teaching learning processes. During this processes there are some things that the teacher will have to bear in mind, this has been narrated in this book. The word assessment has been defined and the various methods of assessment has also been narrated in this book. This book has also mentioned and added a part of information about the assessment and the Right to Education act 2009 where this book also provides a gist of the provisions in Rules under RTE 2009.

A details discussion about the Continuous and Comprehensive Evaluation (CCE) has been done in this chapter of Assessment of Environmental studies at the Primary Level. This book also makes a reference of CCE and other types of Assessment and the need of assessment of the child and a detailed discussion on how assessment of the child can be made. This book discusses the three steps in the assessment of the child which has to be carried out in a cyclic manner and it should be a continuous process. All the three process has been mentioned and described in this book.

In the opening remark itself I have stated that the knowledge of English language is very essential for the children studying in our schools. It is my personal experience that the children who is good in English language would be able to do well in mathematics and science subjects where as other do suffer and really struggle in these subject. I have seen many children do study English language with special classes by paying higher fees and prepare for TOEFL and IELTS so that they get the qualifying grade.

The above example shows how important is English language to the children right from the school level. Though the government has a plan to reduce the status of English stating it as a foreign language, but the desire of the parent is increasing in various states in the country. These days even the northern states are also demanding the teaching of English language.in an era of science and technology we cannot forgo the teaching of English language. This the only language which can help the child to have international contacts and find a suitable job market in any country around the globe.

Learning of language may be any it would provide real excitement, enjoyment and a challenge for the children and the teachers who teach them to create enthusiastic learner. It is our language teacher who mainly help the children to develop positive attitude towards learning of any language. The skills, knowledge and the understanding gained by the children could make a major contribution in the development of the child's oral ability and literacy skills, this also helps the child to understand our own culture, as well as to understand the culture of others in the society. This book also gives an account of the development of English language in our country and how it gradually evolves after independence. It also discusses about the language teaching at primary level.

The most important feature of language learning is the child's ability to read and comprehend text is the center of success in the current and future education. This should also make the child develop an ability to function in the modern society. Every effort is made to understand the ways the children is able to make responses towards the text and about the teaching of the children to write, editing and redrafting and now the use of computer. And effort has been made to understand bilingualism and its effect on the intelligence, cognitive functioning role in the motivation of the children and has thrown light on the evaluation of the English language. I am sure and confident that the reading of this book would be really thrilling and more informative.

Happy good reading.

Dr. Martin Roy Edward
edwardmartin980@gmail.com

About The Author

Dr. Martin Roy Edward has completed his doctorate in Zoology from Dr. Babasaheb Ambedkar Marathwada University, Aurangabad, Maharashtra State. He has completed his post-graduation and graduation from Ahmednagar College, Ahmednagar affiliated with the University of Poona. He has completed his B.Ed. from Annamalai University, Annamalai nagar, Tamil Nadu.

He has completed nearly 40 years in the teaching profession and worked at various capacity in Kendriya Vidyalaya Sangathan and retired on Superannuation from Kendriya Vidyalaya, O.F. Bhusawal, District Jalgaon, Maharashtra State. He is an alumnus of KVS. Now after superannuation he is finally settled down in Visakhapatnam, Andhra Pradesh.

During his service in the Kendriya Vidyalaya Sangathan, he has conducted various experiments in the teaching of sciences and he has got successful results. Apart from that he had a close observation about the children's performance in the class and used to discuss with his fellow teachers and keep a record of his findings and it is this which has helped him to bring out many things in my previous book and in this book. Besides this he is a regular reader of books, magazines, reference materials and the research papers mainly from the nearby college and various University libraries which he usually visits and spend some time reading and writing notes. Most of the research papers are downloaded from the internet for his study.

He was a regular visitor to the nearby private schools and the state government run schools. he has visited number of schools in Maharashtra, Andhra Pradesh, Tamil Nadu, Telangana, and a few in Kerala state. As a result, he has proper experience of teachers teaching in these states and their problems in the urban schools and in the rural area schools of these states. He used to travel more frequently in the rural areas of these states. Now, after retirement, he is confined to the rural areas in the state of Andhra Pradesh. Not only that he is in the managing body of one school in the rural part of Andhra Pradesh and he keeps on regularly visiting this rural school in Andhra Pradesh.

Writing is one of his passion and he has written various articles and delivered several speeches as resource person at various forum. He has presented several papers at various forum. Apart from these he has several Scientific papers which was presented by the author at various National and International scientific conferences. Apart from this he has several papers published in various books and magazines.

His contribution in various fields in social and environmental issues have been recognized and he has been conferred with the honour of "Pariyavaran Rakshak" from the National Council of YMCA of India – Western Region. Further, his prolonged and dedicated service in the field of education has been recognized and was honoured with a Medal and a citation from an organization called North India Sangh, Pune for his contributions in the field of Education, Sports, Music, Social and Culture.

– Dr. Martin Roy Edward

CHAPTER 1

Nature of Science and the Problems of Science Education in India

Let us all be aware of the fact that today we are all living in an era of science and technology, and this has completely changed the life style of all the individuals living in this world. In spite of all these development, even then there is no change in the attitude of mankind. The man has become more and more greedy and selfish. He has been greedily swallowing almost all of the natural resources that is available around him. Today the amount of the natural resources available around him is shrinking and becoming scarce, but the mankind is never bothered about it. There is a steep increase in the basic needs of every individual and that too his demands are steadily increasing in a geometrical ratio. Well it's now high time that we have to think and ponder over the depleting resources and also we have to find out a way for the judicial utilization of our natural resources or we may have to find an alternative source for it. So, that we are able to conserve the natural resources for our future generations. I don't feel that we are able to bring any attitudinal change in the people so that we are able to conserve the natural resources.

I don't think it is right to say that; it's the government's responsibility to see and prevent the destruction of our natural resources that is regularly taking place in our neighborhood, this becomes the duty and the responsibility of each and every individual citizen of our country to act with responsibility against the unruly exploitation of the natural resources. This collaborative and collective effort would bear fruit for us on a long run. No doubt it's the duty of the government of every nation to provide and fulfill the basic needs of its people. One of the major problem is the increase of the population which is increasing day by day in a geometrical ratio. Similarly, in the same way the demands from the people and their expectations are gradually increasing in a tremendous manner, therefore, it becomes the duty of the National Government to take care of its own people and look after the needs of the growing population; as they have to be fed, cared, and looked after, with the limited available earthly resources.

It is very difficult to bring in the attitudinal changes among the mass population in our country this attitudinal changes could be possible only when our population is properly educated. If we are able to take initiative to educate the mass population properly so that they learn the techniques for the judicial use of the available natural resources, thus they should also be educated with the ways how the natural resources could be conserved. It is also very essential that the people of the land should be aware of the various ways of the nature which should be conserved so that the natural resources are never exhausted in nature. The people should also be able to understand and know the effect of depletion of the natural resources in nature. This can be only possible if we are able to provide a strong foundation of science education to our children in our country and these needs to be implemented right from the childhood beginning from the primary school level. A very strong foundation of basic and natural sciences concept has to be developed in them which is the need of the hour. Today, the whole nations in the world is really concerned about our environment and the fast depleting natural resources, and their desires to conserve them so that our children will be able to enjoy the nature and the natural resources and its natural beauty. Hence, today what we need to do is a systematic and a well-planned science education which is essential and this would be the right tool for the development of any nation in the world.

It is this reason that the Science Education has become one of the most important tool for our National Development. Though the country had a very well developed past where the ancient scholars have come out with various scientific discoveries, many may feel that our ancestors were scientifically more advanced and here, I may cite the examples of Ayurvedic science, astrology, Vedic science, yogic sciences etc., but a well-planned science education in the country to the masses has come only after when the country was under the British rule. The systematic and planned Science Education was first introduced in our country by the British. This was way back in

1835 by way of the approval of the Lord Macaulay's minutes, the Science Education has become a common subject in the country with English as the medium of instruction. Ever since the inception of science teaching in the country, there has been tremendous improvement in the standard of living of mankind. There have been improvements in the teaching of science in all the schools and other educational institutions. After independence, the standard of education was further improved by ways of many Education Commissions that came up advocating ways and means to improve Science Education in the country. It was our first Prime Minister Pandit Jawaharlal Nehru who had a vision that Science Education is essential for the development of our Nation and he laid the basic foundations of our country and he also paved the way for Science Education, Scientific Research and Development. It's here I appreciate and consider Pandit Jawaharlal Nehru as a great statesman and a person who had a foresight.

Here I have to say that the Science Education in Independent India has developed well with the production of large number of science graduates and post graduates in the world, this has lead to the brain drain of the talents from our country were the best and the talented graduate and the postgraduates migrate to the United States, Canada and various European countries. The main reason for this is that the Government of India could not provide proper placement for these talented youths. Even though we had the most talented science graduates and postgraduate youth in the country but still we could not see significant growth in the country. This was because of various factors such as, the castes, favourism, and due to corruption, the talents of these youth who were not at all considered suitable for jobs in Indian industries, the Government sectors and in the Research and Development establishments in the country. It has been observed that such students who could not make way in india for employment had migrated in USA, Canada, and the European countries could occupy highest position and do well in those countries and occupy highest position say in industries, R&D and other professions.

It is because of this the number of R&D research publication in India has come down drastically by the end of 80s and it further declined by the end of 90s. To a greater extend the political decisions such as ban on animal dissections at the +12 level and later imposition of ban on animals used for experimentation and trial of medicine's etc. has taken our country at least ten years back in the field of scientific research and science achievement in the country. The enrolment of students seeking admission in all the Engineering branches increased but there was shortage of Engineering colleges, but when the number of Engineering colleges increased then the students were not able to get proper placement in the Government institutes and the Indian industries. Similarly, there was a race for medical admissions in the country but the medical colleges were less in the country. There is an acute shortage of medical doctors in the country now. Similarly, the number of student's admitted in the field of basic sciences is comparatively very low. As a result, the number of students carrying research in the basic sciences is comparatively very less than that of the number of students doing research in Applied Sciences. We should be aware of the fact that for the progress of any country it is mandatory that the country should progress in the field of basic sciences. It is only due to this reason the Government of India came up with the five years integrated basic science degree programme and has built up centers of excellence in various parts of the country. The pettiest part of the whole story is that the seats are limited, selection criteria are tough and the highly talented students are selected. By the end of their study most of them being talented go to other select jobs like the administrative services, railway services and so on. Many of the students are seen settling abroad, and in my thirty-eight years of service I have seen that only the above average students are seen to be going for the Research & Development work. Here I am unable to understand, the reason why highly talented students are admitted and later only a few of them are left for the research in basic science, yes, this is a colossal loss of time, Government exchequer and the tax payers money, instead if we are able to select students above average who are good at study and if they are motivated with innovative ideas would be inclined towards research right from the beginning and these students would sever the country in a better manner after they complete their study in these center of excellence.

There has been lot of efforts made to foster science and technology in our country, but still we are not able to see sufficient development in our country. This may be probably because we are not able to use the adequate required resources for imparting proper education to our younger generation. We are aware of the fact that the seventy percent of the population in our country lives in the rural areas and here they are not able to get the best quality Science Education in our rural areas in our country. It is very essential that we are able to concentrate most of our effort in the rural areas of our country. We should be able to utilize the available resources from our rural areas and apply the same for development, this would certainly change the scenario of our country. The role of teachers in education too also plays an important role in the process of development. However, I feel that the role played by our teachers in India is not sufficient the educational department should put more emphasis and they need to pay more attention on education in the rural areas, by utilizing the available rural resources. The rural teachers should be well trained for teaching in the rural areas properly by utilizing the available rural resources. The role of teachers are needed more in the rural areas and the teachers need to be motivated and well educated and trained in a scientific manner by utilizing all the available rural resources. We will be discussing about the role of teachers in the rural areas in a different chapter separately later.

Even since independence we were concentrating our effort on the development of science education in our country, similarly every effort was made to see that we do well in various fields of scientific research and development. Here once again I would consider the role played by our late Prime minister of India Shri. Jawaharlal Nehru; were he had a vision for the growth of India which was in the direction of Scientific Research and Development. He encouraged late Dr. Homi Jahangir Bhabha to start with the Bhabha Atomic Research Center (BARC) in Trombay. In a similar manner it was the same Prime Minister who encouraged Shri. Vikram sarabhai to start with the Indian Space Research Organization (ISRO). In the same way he is also responsible to dedicate several scientific research centers to the nation. He also had a vision that the Universities in India should take part in the scientific research. The Indian Universities did take part in the scientific research and that can be assessed mainly based on the research publications and the large number of patents filed by the Indian Universities and the other research Institutes in India. However, the rate of publication of the research papers has come down significantly and the reason for this decline in the research papers in the Universities and its affiliated Colleges is due to the political role played by the students and frequent political unrest that occur in the campus of the Universities. The growing pupil indiscipline, unrest among the student community in the Universities and the associated Colleges is a matter of great concern for all in our country.

The growing unrest among the youth is mainly caused due to frustration, because most of the youth in India is highly educated and is unemployed and they are used by the members of the political parties who try to provoke them by giving provocative speech as a result we are able to see youth violence in the country. Further the present youth being educated cannot tolerate favourism and injustice as a result arguments take place and then it leads to violence. If the Government of India is able to provide employment for the youth, then I am sure that no youth would come to help the political wizards to propagate their party ideology for canvassing and they would not be any conflict or violence in the country. The most important thing is that the standard of political canvassing and propaganda has gone to the lowest standard than never before. Sometimes I feel that these youths are been trained by the same teachers of this country they might have been trained to be in disciplined but the political clout for their needs provoke them and make them to enter into violence.

Let's Understand the Nature of Science

Man is known to be a keen observer, he is always curious to know more about his surroundings' and the type of changes taking place around him. He has his own way of thinking, imagination and his own method of enquiry about the study in to the wonders of nature that is occurring around him. As stated above we know that man is a keen observer; since the ancient times he has been trying to analyze about the physical and the biological environment around him and with which he has always interacted; and with an intention to discover new tools so that he could use them to interact with the environment and also understand them and studying carefully. If we are able to go through the book; "A brief History of Science – As seen through the development of scientific instruments" – by Thomas Crump. Would give a brief idea about how science has developed in phases. Man, *Homo sapiens sapiens* is the only species gifted with the power of speech. He can see, hear, touch, taste and smell. It is all these senses which made man to strive and achieve everything for his needs and for his satisfaction. The development of linguistic skill was another very important ability that has been mastered and this has helped him to communicate and express his needs and feelings. The discovery of fire and its use was also mastered by him in spite of the dangers. The art of self-defense has been mastered by him by observing the animals and the birds. The development of modern solar physics and metal technology and so on has been also mastered by him. This effort by man to observe from his surroundings, and he has learnt from the events occurring around him in nature and that can be termed as Science.

Science can be stated to be dynamic; it is an expanding body of knowledge that is able to cover every aspect of new dimensions of human experiences. Now let us try to understand how this knowledge is generated by mankind? What is the methodology he has adapted to seek this knowledge? Let us understand the various scientific method adopted by him? When we are sitting then several complex things come into our mind and many things does occur in our life, and these things can be studies by the use of scientific method, these are the most recognized methods in scientific study. These scientific methods mainly involve several interconnected steps such as observations, looking for regularities and patterns, making of hypothesis, devising qualitative or mathematical models, deducing their consequences; verification or falsification of theories through observations and by carrying out controlled experiments, and then finally arriving at the principles, theories and the laws governing the physical world. There is no strict order of these steps. One may come out and suggest a theory and may also suggest a new experiment or at times our experiment may suggest a new theory or theoretical model. We should be aware of the fact that the laws of science are never viewed to be fixed eternal truth because even the most established and universal laws of science are always regarded as provisional and can be subjected to modification in the light of new observations, experimentation and analysis.

The methodology of science and its demarcation from the other branches of science would be a matter of philosophical debate. The science would profess a value of neutrality and objectivity has they are been subject to critical sociological analyses. Today the science is considered to be at the best peak of its understanding of the simple linear system of nature, however, its predicted or explanatory power is limited when it comes to with the dealing of non linear complex system of nature. Science does have its own limitations and failings, but still science is unquestionable and it is the most reliable and the most powerful knowledge system of the physical world which is known to human today.

Finally, Science is a social endeavor. Science can be considered as a good and an evil master. This is because Science is knowledge and knowledge is power, and with power comes wisdom and liberation. But at the same times science can also breed to arrogance and tyranny. Science does have the potential to be beneficial or harmful, emancipative or oppressive. Today in the twentieth century there are several examples which would speak about the dual role of science. Now the question is how can we ensure that science plays an emancipative role in the world? The answer to this question may lay in a consensual approach to various issues threatening mankind and his own survival today. This may be possible only through the proper exchange of information, transparency and tolerance for various multiple viewpoints. In a progressive society the science may play as a liberating role by helping people to overcome their poverty, ignorance and superstition. Whereas in a democratic political framework, the people themselves can prevent the misuse of science and this would help them to grow and develop themselves in a proper and planned manner.

Understanding the Word Science and Technology

Today, we should be able to understand that more emphasis is given to the teachings of science and technology. This is because that the world is fast changing with new technologies. Therefore, it is essential that one should be aware of the fact that the technology is an applied part of science and its domains are thought to be mechanical, electrical, electronic, optical, and instrumental. The household and commercial gadgets, which come in to the market with the application of chemical, biological, nuclear science, computers, communicative science etc. These are the various types of domains of technology which could be interrelated to one another and they are all derived from the same basic principles of sciences and technology.

As we all know that the Basic Science is an open ended exploration and the end results are not fixed well in advance. However, technology on other hand is also an exploration which is usually done by keeping a definite goal in mind. Technology is a creative process developed from science, as they are, in principle, and infinite ways to reach the definite set goal. Well the technology, makes one creative which may have new ways of designing, planning and charting out the map to the final end conclusion. It is nothing but an innovative application of the known principles of basic science, one should be aware of the fact that the technological solutions are usually guided by proper designing, aesthetic, economic, and other practical considerations by applying known basic scientific principles. As we know that Science is universal, whereas technology is always a goal oriented and often specific to the needs of the local conditions and their requirements.

We should be aware of the fact that the progress of any nation mainly depends upon the nation's advancement in science, science and technology. These advances may lead to an unimagined transformation in various fields which would be beyond our imagination this can be seen in the field of communication, transport, construction, agriculture and in the manufacturing sector. People in our country, today are able to face a fast changing world where they have to develop new skills and adopt themselves to the new demands and creativity to take advantage of the new available opportunities. Therefore; it is essential that we keep all these factors in mind while we plan and shape the science education policy for our nation.

Our Vision of Science Education

After discussing about the nature of science, science and technology; now we are left with one question; that is; what should be our vision of science education in our country? When we are taking this factor into account then we should always consider three important factors into account: first is the learner (the child), second factor is the environment, this involves three factors these are the physical, biological and social life of the child under which the child is always under the influence of all these factors and finally the third; which is the main objective of learning science. Therefore; we should always consider of having a good science education as one that is true to the child, true to life and true to science. These study would naturally lead to some basic criteria for validating the science curriculum as stated in the National Curriculum Frame work 2005 and based on the position paper National Group on Teaching of Science by NCERT (2006) and based on these we have adapted the final vision of teaching science in our country which are stated below:

a) **Cognitive validity:** As per the National Curriculum Frame work, it has been stated that the content, process, language and the pedagogical practices of the curriculum should be properly planned and framed, based upon the appropriate age of the child. This should be planned properly as per the intellectual or the cognitive development of the child's brain.

b) **Content validity:** The content validity should mainly advocate that the curriculum which is framed should be able to convey the contents needed is significantly and scientifically correct. There should always be a simplification of the content material, and it is always necessary to adapt that the curriculum should be to the cognitive level of the child. It is also important to state that, here at this stage utmost care should be taken not to include certain things that is less important and or significant or complex so as to convey some basic things which is flawed and meaningless.

c) **Process validity:** The process validity mainly requires that the curriculum that is framed should be able to properly engages the children in acquiring the various methods and the processes that would lead to the generation and the validation of scientific knowledge, so that we are able to nurture the natural curiosity and creativity in the children towards science and this would help the children in learning science.

d) **Historical validity:** Historical validity is most important and this should mainly advocate that the science curriculum should be properly framed, so that the children are informed about the historical perspective, this would enable the child to appreciate, how the concepts of science have evolved with time. This could also enable the children to view science as a social enterprise and this would influence the children to understand how the social factors also help in the development of science further.

e) **Environmental validity:** The Environmental Validity should mainly advocate that the science should be placed on a wider context of the child's environment, it may be local and global, enabling the children to appreciate the various issues at the interface of science, science and technology and the society, and this would also help in preparing the child and equipping them with the required knowledge, creativity and skills so that they are prepared efficiently to enter the world of work.

f) **Ethical validity:** The Ethical validity mainly requires that the curriculum that has been prepared, needs to promote the values of honesty, objectivity, integrity, co – operation, freedom from all fear and prejudice, and this should also be able to develop among the children a concern for life and help in the preservation of the environment in which they live in. (NCF 2005)

Our Aim of Science Teaching

It is a known fact that science, science and technology do have a significant role to play in the life of mankind. Therefore, the science curriculum should be properly planned, designed and developed mainly based upon the children's interest and as per the requirements of the society. Our aim of formulating the science curriculum should reflect and ponder to all the elements as discussed above. It should also be referred to the changing philosophy of education. We should never forget that science is dynamic and it is fast changing and developing into various disciplines this is mainly due to the very dynamic nature of science.

As per the National Curriculum Framework-2005 (NCF 2005), which states that the science curriculum should have the information of the historical perspective which would show some of the scientific developments, this would provide proper inspiration to the children to read, appreciate and these would also influence the child cognitively, right from the lower classes. In the past the NCERT text books did carry the biographies of some eminent scientists with which the children used to get motivated and posed several questions to the teacher. This has now disappeared from the NCERT text books. Therefore; the science curriculum should also present the developments of science in its various fields and this would benefit to the society and mankind; however; this is a matter of scientific research subject has to how the same can be presented in a manner so that the children are motivated to science and they develop keen interest towards science education.

Our aim of science education should be very closely related to the curriculum and should be based on the policies that are developed for the development of human resources.

This aims as an expression of expectations from the education which includes the people's educational needs and demands (Saylor and et.al., 1981). The needs and demands are very closely related to what they need, and this can be satisfied only by means of education, therefore; whenever we are planning to determine our educational policies, plan them, we need to do the planning of the aims and objectives, then it's very important that we consider the future and plan about what needs to be taken into account. It is important that, here we should mainly focus on various roles the people would play in their near future and it is important that they are made ready for it in the run. Therefore; it is important and essential that we plan our curriculum by keeping a foresight and a vision for the future of the country. We should be very careful in trying to select the content of the curriculum which should be as per the age of the child and the content should be less and the child should not feel that they are overburdened. Every effort should be taken that the child on completion of the study should be confident that he or she would get a proper placement on completion of their studies.

When we are planning the science curriculum, then we should have a clear aim and objectives of science teaching curriculum. The curriculum of science should be properly planned in such a way that it would provide new information to the children that could provoke the children to think again and again with new technological innovations that is required as per the needs of the society. We should be aware of that today the people are living in a society that is based on science and technology, were appliances such as the television, radio, mobiles, computers, laptops, etc., are used by the children in modern education and many appliances are used for the treatment of patients for various diseases such as cancer, heart attacks and so on.

Planning on the future of education should always start by analyzing and reviewing the current situation and its aims and objectives. So for determining the future aims and objectives of science education, we have to plan and think about the future also. Based on this and our requirements we have to predict and these predictions should be taken into account for determining the kind of educational planning that would be required in the future.

It is essential that the teachers should also be involved in the planning of the science curriculum for the future education. Teacher's opinion has to be taken and their views should be considered to be important in the processes of determining the aims and objectives of education. This is important because teachers are closely involved in the implementation and development of the science curriculum.

Our main objective of science education should be to the preparation of a well learned and educated youth or individuals who could work for the society and also provide proper science education. The science curriculum so planned should be aimed to motivate and encourage the students to make them think innovatively and develop the skills to study science, they should be able to learn new skills, they should be able to develop self- confidence, the curriculum thus developed should be able to promote individual and inculcate teams working skills in their respective fields and they should also be able to think in an innovative manner and also develop the required skills for scooping up day to day problems in a systematic manner.

In short; I have to point out that the science education curriculum thus framed should be able to promote among all the children the skills to study science in a proper manner right from the primary school stage to the above levels in the education system. Apart from these the children should be able to develop the following skills as mentioned below:

- The children studying science should be able to develop their own ways for studying habits well planned in a systematic manner.

- The students of science should be able to develop their own skills by putting their own theoretical knowledge into their daily practice.

- The children should be able to gain the required skills by using various tools and equipment's and they should also be able to properly utilize the workshops and the laboratory work in a planned manner.

- The children should be motivated to think and analyze various scientific phenomenon's in terms of their causes – they should be able to develop an effective relationship.

- The children should be able to develop within themselves the skills of creative and innovative thinking.

- The children should be able to attract their attention towards any problems with a planned and a proper scientific study.

- The children should be able to comprehend the relationship between mathematics and science and they should be able to interpret their results in a mathematical form.

- The children should be able to understand and comprehend the ways of obtaining information by going through the research manuscripts and that is available to them in the library or from the internet or those provided to them.

- The children should be able to understand and establish the relationship between the manmade and natural events.

- The children should be able to develop the required skills to cop up with the daily problems faced by them in a proper scientific manner.

- The children should also be provided with the general science knowledge.

- The teaching of science should be done in ways so that it would provoke among the pupil the process of critical and innovative thinking skills.

- The teaching of science should provide the pupil the skills and the knowledge of how to learn.

- The teaching of science should help the children in understanding and comprehending scientific principles and they should be able to explain the principles of nature in a proper manner.

- The teaching of science should make the children to understand the relationship between science and technology.

- The children should be able to carry out scientific experiments and they should be able to reach an inference from the observations and come to a proper conclusion.

- The children should be able to develop the skills of acquiring and using the scientific information.

- The teaching of science should motivate and enable the children to develop the skills of preparing a project either individually or in a team.

- They should be able to comprehend their scientific knowledge that would also form a scientific subject.

- The children should be able to use the problem solving method for understanding and learning of science.

It is clear from the above points that our aim of science education is to see that the children's way of learning science is improved and they should be able to develop the required skills, creative thinking, and they are able to develop innovative ideas and so on. Our basic aim is to see that our children grow and develop into a proper and able citizen who would be able to develop this great nation. The teaching of science should be such that the children are attracted to the science education and enjoy learning science joyfully.

However; it has been seen that in the present days of school teaching is more or less concerned in provide theoretical knowledge instead of giving them first hand practical experiences. In fact, the science teaching should be aimed for a definite class room practice of science. There should always be a very good and healthy interaction between the teacher and the students in the classroom. According to Dewey's active learning method we should have the "learning by doing" and this should be applied in the class room for the teaching of science.

It has been observed by our teachers is that the content level in the science curriculum is high and overloaded this is a most important point which needs to be considered seriously. This creates lot of problems in the student's life in education such as they lose interest and motivation to study science. It is also seen that the child develops fear towards the science subjects and mathematics. Most of the children are scared of mathematics too. This is because both the subject's science and mathematics content in the present school curriculum is very high. It is here comes the talent of the teacher how they teach and create interest and are able to develop the scientific skills among their children to whom they teach. I have been able to see teacher of Mathematics who had adopted a different technique of teaching mathematics which had helped a number of below average children to clear the CBSE public board examination in class tenth. Such teachers would bring in some type of motivation and interest among the children to whom they teach the subject. It would be the teacher's skill how they are able to handle the situation and makes the children feel burden less and motivate them to learn science and mathematics in a fearless environment. Therefore; it is very essential that a systematic approach of teaching science and mathematics should begin right from the lower level i.e., from the primary level this would make a long lasting impact on the child and this would bring joy and happiness among the children to learn science and mathematics.

Finally, what should be our vision of science education? And to summarize this the science education should enable the learner to:

- Know the facts and principles of science and its applications, consistent with the stages of cognitive development.

- The child shall acquire the skills and understands the methods and processes that could lead to the generation and validation of scientific knowledge.

- We should be able to develop a historical and developmental perspective of science and this to enable the students to view science as a social enterprise.

- The children should be able to relate science to the environment, local as well as global, and appreciate the tissue at the interface of science, technology and the society.

- The children should be able to acquire the requisite theoretical knowledge and practical technological skills to enter the world of work.

- The children should develop and nurture the natural curiosity, aesthetic sense and creativity in science and technology.

- The children should be able to imbibe the values of honesty, integrity, humanity, cooperation, concern for life and preservation of environment, and

- The children should be able to cultivate "scientific temper' objectivity, critical and innovative thinking and should develop freedom from fear and prejudice.

CHAPTER 2

Development of Science Education in India

India is the largest democracy in the world and the second largest populous country and it has the second largest education system in the world, but still we are far behind in meeting the basic needs and aspirations of billions of people living in our country. Though; India has the largest education system in the world, but still we are not in a position to control the increasing illiteracy in our country. The illiteracy rate in our country is still hovering around 27%. The female literacy rate in our country is only 64.4%, the male literacy rate in our country is 80.9% this means that the male illiteracy rate is 19.1% and the female illiteracy rate in our country is 35.4%. This goes to say that a lot has to be done in the field of education. There are several states in India, such as Bihar, Arunachal Pradesh and Rajasthan where the illiteracy rate is much higher than that of the national average. It is my observation that all our spending done towards education is not bringing positive results. This goes to show that there is some short falls in our processes of implementation of the educational projects and policies in the country. Therefore, it is essential that we are able to identify the reasons and rectify that and then monitor the implementation of the project and policies for fruitful results.

Science Education – Current Status

On an average the students' access to science education in our country is nearly around thirty percentages. Today we are living in a competitive world. We should be fully aware of the fact that we can excel well in any of the field only if we are able to compete successfully in the interdependent global economy. This can be made possible only if we are having a well-trained man power in Science & Technology. They only can improve the standard of people's living in any country, and this is possible only through proper education. This could be possible only if we are able to make necessary effort by bringing suitable reforms and changes in our curriculum and by updating the same at regular intervals and restructuring various courses regularly right from the school level up to the higher level in science education. Through science education we should be able to provide proper planned training system that could make our students better and more competitive to face the global challenges in the competitive world. If we are successful in doing it, then this would help us to advance well in this globally competitive world economy.

In our country science is usually taught as an integrated subject up to the secondary level. The true discipline oriented science teaching and learning would start only in class XI and XII i.e., by this time the students are at the age group of

16 – 18 years. Though there is a phenomenal increase in the enrolment of students, increase in the numbers of educational institutions, and also an increase in the number of teachers etc. since independence; but still we are far behind from any other advanced countries in the world. If we are able to calculate the enrolment ratio then it is the lowest enrolment ratio is far lower in science education as compared to the corresponding figures of the developed countries like the USA, UK, and Germany etc. this goes to show that our science education has to go a long way to reach its destination.

TABLE - 1

Percentage enrolment in various disciplines at graduate level in Higher Education 2015-16.

Disciplines	Graduation	Post graduation	Ph.D.
Arts/Humanities/Social Sciences	40.08%	12.54%	17.52%
Engineering and Technology	15.57%	24.19%	6.65%
Science	16.04%	24.25%	13.00%
Medical Sciences	3.30%	4.14%	3.33%
IT & Computers	2.50%	2.10%	6.22%

Data Source: Department of Higher Education, MHRD, Government of India

If we are able to take into consideration about our students belonging to the age group from 5 – 18 years in our country, this age group corresponds to the student from classes I to XII. It's observed that more than 50% of the student population remains out of the school by the end of class tenth. Similarly, if we consider the students from the age group 17 – 18 years, then we can see that only 25% – 35 % is having access to education, this means that nearly 65% – 75% of students are out of the school immediately after the first public examination. Most of them are either failed or they are permanently out of the educational system. A study conducted has also shown that most of the students, who fail at the class tenth public examination, most of the students are seen failed mainly in mathematics and science. This leads to a colossal loss and wastage of human effort and the public money that is caused due to the student's failure. In the same way, if we consider the number of students, who drop out of the school education midway in the school system, is due to failure or due to repetition, here to this is also seen due to failure in science and mathematics. This shows a very poor and a sorry state of science and mathematics education in our country and this also shows the type of teaching that is prevailing in our country, at the school level, and by seeing this it is important and necessary that something needs to be done at the school level as soon as possible to see that the teaching of science and mathematics is properly improved right from the primary stage of our schooling up to the secondary level. If this is the state of our school education, were the number of school dropouts is increasing, then where do we stand; nowhere, but as per the constitution were we have pledged to provide free and compulsory education to all the children up to the age of 14 years. This dream has been shattered and for this we will have to improve the quality of education in our country so that all the children get proper education up to class tenth.

Science Teaching – Problems

If we were to consideration the students admitted to our schools right at the primary school level and up to the secondary school level. We will be surprised to see that these students who enter into our educational system are with full of vigor, zest, vitality and curiosity. But the saddest and the sorry state of our educational institution in our country is that our teachers teaching at our primary or at the elementary school level and up to the secondary school level are not able to maintain the same level of zest, vitality and curiosity among these students throughout their study in the school level, or they try to make an effort to see that the child's sense of curiosity, interest, are maintained. If they are able to do so, then the interest of the students entering into the primary or elementary school level and the secondary school level should have been maintained well. However, the saddest part of the whole story is that the teaching at the elementary school level and the secondary school level is so poor that the students lose their interest in science and mathematics and they start developing hatred and fear towards these subjects. The inborn talents of the child to question the teacher and to know and understand about things that are occurring around them is really suppressed and crushed by our own teachers in the school. This result in suppressing the children own open mindedness and his quest for knowledge is also crushed off. As a result, the children lose their interest towards these subjects and tries hating them. This also effects directly on the growth of the child and suppresses the child's built in desire, quest, interest and attitude towards his thinking and creativity.

The present studies also show that the condition of school teaching in the primary and in the secondary school is very poor in the rural areas of the country, as we all know that the majority of our population live in the rural areas. The educational boards, the state and the central board of secondary education try to boost their educational results with the urban lot and the rural lot of students. If they are directed to separate the urban and the rural school results separately then the true scenario of the student's performance would come out and then we would be able to do the required remedial measures so that the rural educational institutes could also be improved. Today what's happening is that the results of the board examination are good so more and more concentration is put on the urban lots for the improvement of the results and the rural education institutes were the larger portion of the country's population is studying is really ignored. Due to this a large concentration of talented children in the rural areas are not able to come for competition with the urban students.

The only way; which I feel to improve the standards of education in the rural areas, this could be done only if we are able to make the Central and the State Educational Boards to declare their results separately for urban and the rural area schools. When the results in the rural area is poor or it declines then there would be some momentum in government arena to improve the rural area results also. This effort by the government would certainly increase the percentage of results in the rural areas also. This effort made by the government agencies would certainly improve the quality of education in the rural areas, as a result there would be an improvement of board results in the rural areas. It is also understood that the poor performance of education in the rural areas is due to the corrupt practices of the rural level education officers of the state, who also has the responsibility to inspect the rural areas schools and is also responsible for improving the quality of education in the rural areas. Now if we need that the status of rural schools has to be improved, then the only way is that the rural level education officers should be made accountable.

The real plight of the students living in the rural areas of our country is that they don't have a proper school and if there are schools then we don't have proper qualified teachers to teach these subjects. The condition of the Government schools and the private schools are the same in most part of the country. To some extend the private school are better than the Government Schools, the present Governments policy of not providing grants to the private schools and English medium teaching private schools in the country has further worsened the situation. The Government should at least provide grant for the teacher's salary so that the teachers teaching in the rural areas could be made accountable. The other problems are that it is very difficult to get a qualified teacher in the rural areas. In most of the rural school we don't have good qualified teachers teaching science and mathematics to the students. This mainly leads to most of the failure of students in the public examination, and this leads to school drop outs at various levels of their school education. The most vulnerable group is the girl students who drop out of the school education in most of the states. This is because that most of the states such as Bihar, Jharkhand, Rajasthan, chatisghad, and some parts of Uttar Pradesh and Madhya Pradesh, people still feel that the girl's education is not important and this is due to the lack of proper motivation among the population. It is also seen that most of the rural schools are not equipped with proper science labs etc., where the children could carry out some experiments so that they are able to fulfill the desire of experimentation to explore their surroundings and fulfill their quest for knowledge.

Promotion of Effective Science Teaching

Teaching of science, it may be at any level of education it should be well planned and communicated to the students in a very simple and in an exciting manner. It should be done in such a way that the teacher teaching of science should really provoke a sense of rational thinking among the students and this sense of rational thinking and the sense of keen observation should develop within them. However, it is my common observation that the teaching of science is not done in the way they have to be done. In most of the schools throughout the country, this include both urban and the rural schools in India where science is taught as prose and poetry by just reading the text and without giving proper explanation or communication given by the teachers to the students, the real sense of excitement of learning science comes off from doing things which is not found in our country. In most of the schools it is also seen that the science teacher make the students read the science text book as it is done in language teaching, and make the students learn science by rote or by giving them notes by dictation. The students are not taught science by participating or by doing science. The students are not made to explore things and then understand science and the laws of nature, but they are given laws of nature by definition and the principles of scientific facts are given to them in writing in the form of notes, apart from that they are given answers of the question given at the end of each chapter on the black board and then the children are made to memorize and mug up these answers by heart by rote method. One should be able to understand that science is an endless quest of unceasing exploration which should be embraced and fostered in a natural way by proper explanation, properly communicating science, experimentation and observation, but the pettiest part of all our schools is that the students are forced to learn science by heart by rote. By doing so our students are not able to develop the sense of curiosity, innovative ideas, provocative thinking, etc., by which they are likely to lose interest towards the learning of science, and they would not be able to understand the basic concepts of all the scientific laws of nature.

It is our common observation in most of the schools, whether it may be urban or rural the teachers, teaches science by reading out the science text book. The teacher gives no explanation to the students. It has also seen that the teacher provides the answers of the question those which are given at the end of the chapter on the black board. The student's barely copy down the same and they have to study these questions by rote method. Facilities such as the teaching aids are available in the school, a very good equipped laboratory is also available in the school, but they are not at all used in the daily class room teaching. Sometimes it has been observed that the students tell their science teachers to take them to the laboratory, but the teacher's simply ignore their demand. The reason probably very well known to the teacher alone or may be that the teacher has to prepare the laboratory arrangement and plan the experiment well in advance or prepare the write up which the teacher will have to hand over to the students well in advance, so the students are also prepared for the lab activity. This act by the teacher would discourages the child's zeal and quest towards the knowledge and his interest for the study of science and their ability to think and imagine thus enabling them to bring their original innovative ideas into reality by applying their own skills. The students' needs to be motivated to read and learn science by understanding science in a proper manner, so that they are able to imbibe the basic concepts in a proper manner.

It was seen in the past that the NCERT text books used to carry the information about great men of science and the scientist who had contributed their might and discovered phenomenon or any law in science. A brief history and their contributions were narrated. This information's provided about the scientist were the real aspirations and motivation for the students at the school level. I have seen some students questioning their teachers about it. These days this information is missing in the NCERT text books so that the student were not able to get the real inspirations from this information about the great men of science and how they worked. It is very essential that our students in our schools should be taught about how these great men of science discovered various natural laws by exploration and experimentation. For example, an apple fell on Sir Isaac Newton's head, and that lead him to the discovery of Newton's Law of Gravitation. Similarly, how Sir Thomas Alva Edison sat on the eggs to hatch them, when he was told by his mother that the hen sits on the eggs for hatching chickens etc. this gives an indication to the students that the teaching of science can be only done through exploration, curiosity, imagination and for the development of curiosity, the students should be provoked to think, think and again think, but this is very rarely seen in our countries school science education. It is because of this Dr. A.P.J. Abdul Kalam always tells the children to think, think and keep thinking.

Curiosity is one of the inborn characteristic which is possessed by each and every child, but this inborn talent which every child has; and this curiosity which needs to be properly nurtured, fostered and motivated by our teachers in the school. But it is seen that these very our own teacher in the school are seen to crush and kill the inborn characteristics which the child possesses by the present system of Science Education in our school. It has been observed in the lower classes specially in the primary classes every child has the tendency of asking questions, this may be out of curiosity or may be to know more about the things happening around them, but most of their questions are never answered to the students by the teachers, but on the other hand the child is discouraged, scolded, threatened and at times the child is made as a laughing stock in front of the class by our teachers in the schools. The same thing happens for our children at home also, because most of the parents are not in a position to answer the child's questions because most of the parents are uninformed of the questions so they are unable to answer or they are uneducated. Under such conditions, the child has only one option and that is to present their doubts as question to their teachers. In most of the schools I have observed that the teachers avoid answering the student's questions. This makes the student feel that the teacher is either unaware of the answer or the teacher is avoiding to provide the correct answer. Thus the doubt raised by the child remains in his mind and it remains unclear.

Here, I wish to point out that most of the teachers in our school are not able to understand the main objectives of the children asking questions. The teachers should be made to understand that the basic objective of asking question by a child, this is the first and the primary step towards the acquisition of knowledge. This is one of the vital steps towards the child's acquisition of knowledge. These questioning not only denotes the child's ignorance, but it also reflects their keen desire to know the facts and their desire to understand the things that is occurring around them. Here the teacher should be able to understand that questioning is one of the most basic criteria for the child's acquisition of knowledge, and being a teacher it's important that we should know this fact and it becomes the duty of the teacher to satisfy the child's by answering his questions. We should also know the fact that the eminent scientists too have questioned and this has led to great discoveries. For example; Sir Thomas Alva Edison as a child sat on the eggs to hatch them only after asking his mother a question; why does the hen sit on the eggs? This was a question put forth by him out of curiosity. Similarly, the Indian Scientist Sir C.V. Raman questioned himself; why is the ocean blue? To seek an answer to this question he ended up discovering the Principles of Raman Effect. Similarly, Prof. Albert Einstein who stood in front of the mirror and questioned himself; what will I be able to see, if I would run towards the mirror at the speed of light? This question leads him to the discovery of the Theory of Relativity. In short, what one has to think is that, by asking questions a child is expressing his ignorance and at that time if the teachers are able to answer them then, this means that the teachers are not able to expand the child's horizon of knowledge. This type of act by the teacher would help them to develop an interest among the students towards the subject science, not only that the child would be tempted to ask more and more questions by doing so the child shall be encouraged to expand his own horizon of knowledge. A good teacher can encourage the child to read more information on the topic from a text book by providing the same to them. This would encourage the child and they would develop the habit of reading with an objective of acquiring additional knowledge on the subject.

Today, I am very sorry to say that the teaching of science in our schools have become duller and more uninspiring, more or less it is done only by chalk and talk method. Yes! It is essential that we should be able to understand that the journey of learning science is very exciting and a fascinating journey provided if it is done properly. However; the spirit of exploration which was once, used to form the very core of learning science is now disappearing totally from our schools. Today, what is happening in our schools is that more emphasis is put on teaching by ramming science rather than making them learns by understanding, by reasoning and finding out answers by doing it themselves. The conceptual way of teaching science is no more seen in most of the schools. Today during the process of science teaching in which the student is never informed about the true excitement of doing science, Today, for most of the children learning science has become a great burden and they also feel learning science is very difficult, rather than an exciting adventure to understand nature. This has led to an increased hatred towards the science subject, as a result many students are seen giving up this science subject and today as a result of this there is an increase in the school dropouts at various levels in the school. A great number of students are seen failing in science and mathematics subjects in their first public examination.

Today we are living in an era of science where there is tremendous explosion of knowledge in the field of science and technology. Accordingly, our system of science education should change and we should be able to gear up to teach more and more scientific concepts in a lesser time, no wonder whether the children are able to understand, what is been taught to them. The children are taught so fast these days that the teacher never bothers to ask whether the children have understood the topic what have been discussed and taught to them. There are certain instances where the children do not get sufficient time to ponder into what they have been taught by their teacher in the class room. This goes to show that, the present system of education has nothing to do, whether the students are nourished or nurtured with creativity, skills, innovations or whether the teacher is able to promote as a model building capacity among the children in the present day system of science education. The teachers have their own explanation that the syllabus is more and it has to be completed in time so that the student can be given more time for practice for the examination.

Another most important factor is that teaching of science in most of our school is mainly examination oriented. Today, we have an examination system which I don't think that it is been designed properly in a scientific manner. This does further complicate the situation this is because the examination and evaluation does not have any correlation between science education and its evaluation. If we are able to consider the evaluation of science at the secondary and senior secondary level, this seems to be totally mechanical type of testing where I feel that our examination system tests the ability of our students to memorize and reproduce the answers of specific set of questions in the examination. It looks like that our examination system is designed in such away so that we are able to prepare students who are capable to produce children who could reproduce answers mechanically just like robots who are able to answer selective set of questions, that to the answers which they give is similar to those given in their text books or student guides which has now become popular and it has been seen that these guides are used by the teachers also in their class room teaching.

Setbacks in Science Education

One of the greatest problems with the present day student generation is that they after coming out of our educational institutions they are not able to apply their acquired knowledge to any unknown situation and sort it out. This is mainly because the examining body i.e., examining board whether central or the state Board every year they come out with sample question papers, guide books and other text under the nomenclature stated as guide material or student support materials and this gives an idea to the well experienced teacher about the nature of the questions paper that would to be asked in the board examination or most likely questions and accordingly selective teaching is carried out by our teachers in the schools. That means there is selective teaching and selective learning occurring in these days and the same is also seen as a common phenomenon in nearly all the schools under the board examinations in the country. Due to this system of teaching and learning the students are not in a position to retain what they have learnt and they easily forget what is learnt because the basic concepts of any topics in science is not understood by the students. The students don't learn science by doing science, hence the chance of retention is very less. Thus to improve the standard of education in our country we need to stop the practice of providing the sample papers, printing of guide books etc.

It is because of this type of mechanical system of examination, today we are able to see the large scale mushrooming of several coaching classes in each and every city in our country. The numbers of coaching classes are more in cities where the state board or the central board offices are situated, and most of the students are seen going to attend these classes. Many students are confident that maximum questions appearing in the board examination may be from the sample paper provided by their coaching classes tutor, and the fees charges by the coaching class tutor is also very heavy which all the students are not able to pay. Most of the tutors running classes in the cities where board offices exist might be having some type of links or contacts with the officials of the board hence they are able to make up a proper guess paper for their students. Further they are also able to guide the students, how to answer these question? They also put more emphasis on the technique of writing answers in the examination. Due to these reasons the children are now seen visiting coaching classes in each and every town. They are also seen running from one coaching class to another coaching class right from the early hours in the morning to late night, thus putting tremendous physical and mental stress on the children which becomes totally unbearable leading to physical and psychological breakdown. To keep a check on this situation it's essential that we bring reforms in the examination system and that of evaluation of science this needs to be taught properly and the teaching of science to be taken about very seriously.

Today the situation is such that the number of students opting for science stream admission at the school level in class eleventh and twelfth is fast declining in almost all the schools and the Junior colleges in the country. Whereas, in some reputed institutions such as Kendriya Vidyalaya Sangathan, Navodaya Vidyalaya Samiti, and some State boards institutions etc., has put up cut off marks for seeking admissions for science stream. This has made many students disappointed; especially those who are really interested in studying science but are not allowed to seek admission. During my vast years of teaching experience, I have come across numerous students who had secured less mark in mathematics and science in the tenth board examination and they have sought admission in science stream and they have done very well and are holding very good positions and working as well-known scientist, engineers and doctors. I have seen and also; am of the opinion that the talent of the child really opens up when they are provided the subject of their own choice, so that they are able to excel well in their own field of interest. But I see that this concept has not reached in our country. The burecrates who formulate the countries education policies is not able to digest this part, but they try to classify the children based on the mechanical system of evaluation of our education system which is carried out by the examining body the board, where there is selective teaching. However, my observation is that the children who get less mark have most of the basic concepts clear as compared to the merit holders who run from one coaching center to another and scores more marks. And I have experienced that the students who scores less marks in the board examination and those who are not in merit do well in the science subjects in years to come.

I have been able to see that the students in some parts of Maharashtra scores very good marks in the board examination and always tops in the Poona Divisional secondary and higher secondary Board examination every year. This was the headline news every year immediately after the declaration of the results. It was later found out that the students who score high marks and top the examination could not stand in the competitive exams and they could not do well in their further studies. The reason which was found out later that the students of class X and XII in this region of Maharashtra state the parents sent their children to the coaching classes and when the students are in class XI, then these students were taught the syllabus of class XII. The same syllabus is repeated once again when these children are in class XII. So the children are given training twice for the same syllabus of class XII and those children studying in class X also get training for class X twice. These children are drilled again and again on the same syllabus for two years keeping in mind with the examination point of view. Thus these children never had any of their basic concepts clear of the fundamental science of class XI & XII. So these children could not do well in any of the competitive exams and later in the professional colleges say medical or in engineering colleges they could not do well so they fail and take more years to complete their medical and engineering courses due to back log. They are not successful doctors or proper engineers as they lack the basic concepts of science. It has been seen that very less children are seen to work hard and try to acquire the basic concepts and do well in their study of science. This system was popularly known as the Latur system of education, as this type of educational practice was done in Latur district of Maharashtra state. This type of education would produce proper results in the examination but they are not able to produce real scientific talents who would do some good for the future of our nation.

Steps Undertaken to Promote Science

Today efforts are made by the Government of India to lure the students towards the study of basic sciences. For this reason, the National Council for Educational Research and Training (NCERT) introduced the National Talent Search examination (NTSE). The scheme was to provide scholarships to the nationally selected students depending upon their performance in a carefully designed test. This scheme provided scholarships to those students who choose to take science as their career, but those students who performed well and showed outstanding performance in science but later dropped out from science and opted for non – science or other professional courses instead of basic science. This shows that large number of the students does not want to take science as their career; the reason is that they don't find science to be a lucrative career.

The Department of Science and technology (DST) too has also introduced a new scholarship scheme to encourage the young talented students to take to science as their career and encourage them by providing them facilities to nurture and motivate these young students in the field of scientific research in this country. It was with this motive the department of science and technology has introduced the Kishore Vigyan Protshahna Yogana (KVPY). The basic aim is to select the best talented student with the scientific skill and innovative ideas in any field of basic sciences and nurture them in good research organizations such as the Indian Institute of Sciences (IISc) Bangalore. For which the DST conduct a national wide examination along with an interview which is carefully designed to find out talented young brains to head the countries future research.

All this effort by the government of India in the field of science education was mainly to lure the talented young brains to lead the counties future basic scientific research. At the same time, we also face serious threat to the science from people within our own country. The step motherly attitude developed and propagated by our political leaders against the English language in some parts of our country has invariably effected the propagation and education of sciences. English is an International language mainly used for the propagation of science and scientific literature throughout the world.

The other main and most important factor is that most of our population in the country is living in the rural areas. We have a very good and intellectual lot of talented youth residing in the rural parts of our country, these students are not able to come up and compete with their counterpart youth in the urban areas of our country. Thus we are losing a good number of very young talented youth who are not able to come and compete in the science learning. These students would be good and their talents could also be used for the scientific research in our country. If their talents are properly used, then they could bring revolution in our rural areas and this would seriously have affected our growth of science in our rural areas in the country. The reason for the backwardness of the most of the talented youth from the rural background who are not able to come up and do well in the science education because they are very poor in English. The reason is that these students in the rural areas of our country is not taught English at the school level. It is my observation that a few students who manage to study in the rural areas and go to the college in the urban areas and graduate themselves are treated as alien because they are not good in English and these students are ridiculed by their professors in the college and they are not able to cope up with the situation and these students greatly sufferer or leads a frustrated life in the future as they are not able to withstand the competition along with their counterparts in the urban background. Now the question is why there is dual policy in education? Why does the students in the rural and the urban are discriminated and why they are not treated alike? It is my observation in most of the rural areas in the states of Maharashtra, Tamil Nadu, Karnataka, Kerala, and Andhra Pradesh the children are most talented and if they are provided proper education as provided in the urban areas then these students would be an asset for the counties future and its development. Among these states some of them has started English education in the rural areas right form the primary level and the students are doing well and the result would be good and we will have to wait and seen the transformation this would make in the near future.

The other treat for our science education comes from the handful of people who really oppose scientific experimentation on animals. The strong opposition from some politicians to ban dissections at school has resulted in loss of students interests towards biological sciences. Further the teaching of body systems however, has to be demonstrated by any electronic media which will not attract the child. But the real curiosity of learning science by doing and this basic concept is failed here. The child also has a lot of questions to ask when an animal is dissected and when he really touches the different internal organ and feels it and this motivates them. By stopping dissection in schools and other education institutions is only to show their strength and authority and this act has really killed the curiosity of the children and their ability to understand the body structure and its internal organs in a better way. Banning the use of animals for basic research has taken the country about ten years back in our basic scientific research in our country, however some amendments have been done for the use of animals in the basic scientific research in the country.

CHAPTER 3

Begin Teaching Science from Early Childhood Years

Have you ever witnessed a child playing near the sea shore or in an open field, if so, you might have seen the child picking up small stones, pebbles, shells, and collecting them? Similarly, you might have also seen the children collecting different sizes of leaves, etc. from the garden and might have seen the children trying to segregate them and trying to arranging these things according to their colour, size and shape. You might have been surprised to see them doing it; and at that time you might have even felt, how they could decide to do it and who has taught them to do it? The answer should be very simple, nobody has taught them, but it's the child's basic instinct which has made him to do so. If you are a keen observer, and if you could have seen that when the young one of an animal is born then the newly born sibling of these animals has the ability to stand up themselves and go to the mother for suckling of the milk. The human siblings are not able to get up and walk as like the other animal siblings could do. Our careful observation on the growing child could reveal a lot of things, about their behavior, movements, their likes and dislikes etc. We will be able to learn a lot about the child's behavior right from their infancy. What is seen is that the infants are able to learn many things by observing things happening around them in their own home environment as they grow. Now by this time we would be able to understand that every child has its own basic instinct that is already within the child and this makes the child play like this as what is mentioned above in my this opening statement.

Some infants are seen to catch and pulling out the earthworm from the borrow when they see the earthworm moving. They also want to know how the earthworm moves and they will enjoy by seeing how the earth worm struggle and moves. Similarly, some infants are seen trying to catch the fast-moving black ants and at times the child is seen screaming loudly this is when the black ant bites them and this causes them pain. Thereafter, it is observed that the child will never touch the black ant, but the child will start screaming when the black ant would approach the child or whenever the child see's the black ant. Have you ever seen the children playing with the puppy or with a kitten? No doubt, it is very interesting to see when the child keeps on playing with these animals. But if the child sees an adult dog which barks at the child then the child will go away from the dog. Thereafter, when the child sees a dog then the child will start crying. In short; what I wish to convey is that the young child is always engaged with their own surroundings where the child is living this involves both living and nonliving things. In short, the child would be much more engrossed in the environment where the child lives in. This would involve various types of activities and the various phenomenon's that are occurring in the child's immediate environment by experiencing it and by observing it as the child grows. The child would also be trying to build a scientific idea by some sort of scientific thinking or they may try to develop a scientific process in such a way that they are able to develop their own skills of observation, classifying and sorting things and displaying whatever they have collected in their own ways and means. So, these are the some of the scientific skills what the child keeps developing in their own ways during the early stages of infancy to till the child attains the age of toddler. In fact, I should say that the small children do have the basic instinct of identifying things in a proper manner and grouping them and classifying them. This skill which exist in the child needs to be nurtured and cared for and should be brought up properly by our teachers right from our kindergarten and the school in a systematic manner. It is from this, the concept of the phenomenon of Back to Basics has been derived and developed.

Importance of Science teaching in the Early Childhood Education [ECE]

Several research studies carried out in the field of developmental and cognitive Psychology has proved that the environmental surroundings in which the child lives would effect a lot and they are more important during the early years of infancy and this decides and bring the requisite change in the child and this has a long lasting effect on the child's development. It has been understood that if there is a lack of needed stimuli to the child then; this may result in the child's development without the child reaching to their full potential. Therefore, science education in the early childhood education does have a greater importance in many aspects of the child's development. This has been suggested by researchers who states and concludes that science education should begin right from the early years of schooling.

There are several reasons which has been pointed out, as to why the teaching of science should start right from the early years of childhood education.

1. We all as teachers and we should be aware of the fact that, every child does have a natural basic instinct or they have a natural tendency to enjoy by observing their immediate surroundings and thinking about the objects around the child and the nature around him, further we should be aware of the fact that the child as they grow they are also a keen observer of all the events that are happening around them.

2. We as teachers should be aware of the fact that the young children should always be motivated to observe and explore the world around them, and this should be the first and the early science experiences which the child should be able to capitalize as they grow.

3. It is important that utmost care should be taken to see that the children are properly engaged with the best

quality of science learning experiences which is a very vital issue right from the young age and this would help the children to understand the world around them. The children should also be encouraged well so that they would be able to collect and organize things and information themselves in a better way and they should also be able to test new ideas and the child should be able to develop a positive attitude towards science learning right from the young age.

4. We teachers should be very clear that the quality of science learning experiences that needs to be provided to the child, should be of a high standard and we should be able to provide a solid foundation for the child's development in science right from the Early Child Education, we should also help the child for the development of the scientific skills and the concepts development among the children which they could encounter throughout their academic career in their life.

5. It should be very clear that the teaching and learning provided to the children, they should be able to construct a proper understanding of the key science concepts and this should also allow and encourage them for the future learning of more abstract ideas in sciences.

6. It becomes the duty of the teacher to see that the children are made to engage and with scientific knowledge and

they get the required science experiences right from their childhood and this would also allow the children to develop scientific skills and critical thinking.

7. Make sure that the children should be properly supported and motivated by the teachers for the development of the scientific, critical thinking and skill development among the children right from their early childhood years; this could also guide and lead the children for an early transfer of their thinking skills to other academic domains which may also support their academic achievement and enhance their sense of self efficacy.

8. Now by providing an early childhood science learning it is very important to address the achievement gaps in the science performance. It is through these the achievement gaps in science can be slowly narrowed. However, these achievement gaps may still exist between grade level and time, this can also be seen with respect to the race/ethnicity, socio-economic status and gender parity.

9. These achievement gaps in the science subject will always be "alarmingly congruent over time and across various studies". These achievement gaps are clearly evident right at the very start of the school. As per the studies carried out in the United States of America, it has been observed that the achievement gaps are evident at the time of enrolment for the science course,

college majors and career choices. This achievement gaps is also seen to persist across racial/ethical groups, socio – economic status and gender parity. (National Science Foundation, 2001, 2002). To some extend this seems to be true in our country also but a detailed study is required on this issue. Scholars have also linked that the early difficulties faced by the students in learning school science and their decisions not to pursue advanced degree and careers in science. This is also a common problem seen in our schools also.

10. All effort made by our teachers towards science education and its reforms should mainly aim for education of "Science for all students". Here we should be able to bridge the Science achievement gaps. We need to develop a proper systematic instructional framework right from the early childhood science education. It should also be noted that any insufficient curriculum which is not properly linked to the required standards and if it is not provided with an inadequate teaching resource, then we will never be able to add and attach the required goals without a proper curriculum.

11. We should be aware of the fact that a poor level of science teaching at an early childhood year would mainly contribute to a negative students' attitudes towards science and this may lead to a very poor performance of the child, and this problem may continue to persist into the middle and high school years also in the child's

education (Mullis and Jenkins, 1988). Therefore; it is essential that the teaching at the ECCE should be done with a proper planned curricula and a proper planning is required for teaching science to the children in the ECE. If we fail to do so, then its effect can be seen in the children up to the high school stage.

12. Here, I have to state that the various studies carried out also suggested that an effective and a positive early science teaching and experiences would help the children to develop a proper scientific concepts, proper scientific reasoning and the required scientific skills, they will also learn to associate themselves with peers in carrying out various activities and they will develop cooperative learning skills and this will also help them to develop a positive attitude and interest towards science and they will understand science by really performing science by performing experimentation. This would really lead to a better foundation for the development of all the scientific concepts that the child needs to be studied at a later stage in their education.

Developing the Idea of Science in Children at An Early Stage

In order to understand the development of an early idea of teaching science among the children of the early childhood group, and to understand that it becomes essential that we are able to learn the ways how the children are able to visualize things and then try to understand and learn the various concepts of science. To do this it is important that we should be able to understand the children's point of view to know about how the children visualize their surroundings about what they see around them. We should be able to understand that there are number of factors that is influencing the children's understanding of the various scientific concept on the various natural phenomenon's that are occurring around the child. If we are able to keep a constant watch on our children's activities carefully, then we can observe and learn their role in nature, here we would be able to understand their own potentiality to develop their own concepts this would depend upon their own experiences which they would gain through their own observations and experiences. The child's concepts which they develop may not be scientifically correct or sometimes their ideas may not be based on the real scientific concepts or ideas, and or it cannot be ignored; these can be referred as an "alternative concepts". Here I would like to refer to Dust and Treagust (1995) who has proposed six possible sources for alternative conceptions and these are – *sensory experiences, language experiences, cultural background, peer groups, mass media and even the science instructions.*

Now if we are able to think and consider about our children's point of view on natural sciences, then it could be mainly based on the child's understanding of the scientific concept and this may also depend upon how the child is able to view and think about our nature. The children should always be encouraged to view things in a self-centered or in a human – centered perspective. They can also be seen to attribute human characteristics such as feelings, will or purpose to objects and phenomenon (Piaget, 1972, Bel, 1993).

If we are able to see the children's way of thinking, then it seems to be perceptually dominated and usually it is limited in focus. In most of the cases the children are seen to focus on various changes rather than the steady state conditions, this would make it difficult for them to recognize the patterns on their own without the help of others knowledgeable peer groups or the adults (Inagaki, 1982).

It is always seen that the children's concepts that is developed by them are mostly undifferentiated, that is, the children sometimes may make use of labels for the concepts in a broader or narrower ways that may also have some different meanings than those used by the scientists (Driver et.al., 1985, Inagaki, 1992).

It is seen that most of the children may use the concepts of labeling the living and non-living things differently than what the adults do. For instance, most of the children consider the plants as non-living things because most of the young children feel that the plants don't move, however, it has been observed that some children do consider some non- living things; such as the clouds as living things. This is because for these children the cloud appears to be as moving in the sky, similarly, some children consider the car as a living thing as they move from one place to another. In short, we can conclude that the child's view, ideas and their application of mind and their knowledge mainly depends upon the context in which the children are used to it (Bar and Galits, 1994; Driver et.al., 1985).

It can also be understood that the children's views are mostly stable even after things are being formally taught in the class room, it is usually seen that the children do not show change in their views or ideas despite the teachers makes attempt to challenge their views and ideas by offering a counter evidence. It is also seen that most of the children ignore the counter – evidence or they would interpret the evidence in terms of their own prior ideas which they have (Russell and Watt, 1990; Schneps and Sadler, 2003).

How the Teaching of Science Be Done Effectively in These Children?

If we consider the contemporary instructional approaches that are described in our science educational literature, then this can be considered as constructive philosophy. If it is so, then we should be able to consider all the forms of constructivism, and all the forms of instructional applications should also be treated as constructivism. Under these conditions it can be seen that the children can also play as a very crucial and significant role as an active agent for their personal acquisition or construction of their knowledge (Fornor, 1996; Gunstone, 2000). It is all these instructional approaches which would aim to promote active learning among the children through the use of hands – on –activities in small groups and this would also help in a sense of making our children to discuss issues among themselves. It can also be expected that our children would be able to construct and develop a proper understanding of the science context about our environment around them in a proper way by using the inquiry based learning technique.

Here as a teacher teaching science subject it become our moral duty to provide a minimal guided instructional approaches to these children who are involved in the process of study of their own environment. This may have a heavy burden on the child's cognitive processing, and at times this may also tend not to be that effective for these young children. If we are able to provide a heavy cognitive burden to these children, then they would be left with a very little capacity with these children to process the novel information gained by them, thus hindering in their learning activity. However, most of the teachers who are teaching these children do believe and consider that these young children do have a very limited cognitive processing capacities, for an inquiry based instructional approach. Now in this case if these children are properly guided by our teachers, then this would have been a better offer and a most effective way to engage these young children to learn new science concepts in their own ways in the school environment.

If we have a well-planned and a properly guided inquiry based instructional approach for teaching science, then this would usually allow and help our children in the building of the new scientific concepts, with this the child would be able to use their acquired knowledge with their existing mental model, this will also help them to utilize the same knowledge to develop their own new activities. Where as in a guided inquiry approach, the children are expected to be an active member or an agent in the learning of various activities, this would really help the child to strengthen the children's sense of ownership of their own work and this would also enhance their zeal and motivation towards the understanding of the new science concepts. If we are able to continue with this type of systematic and planned approach with these children; when they are usually working in small groups, then this would also promote their collaborative skills and this will also provide opportunities for these children to help in building the peer's understandings. This means that the science activities thus planned should have relevance to the children's daily lives, thus this would allow children to make connections between what they already know and what they are learning.

These Sense-making discussions would really promote children's awareness about the learning and the development of concepts and this would also facilitate them in restructuring of an alternative ideas into a constructive, development of science mental models.

We are all aware of the fact that the teachers are involved in working with our children, the main purpose is to enhance and develop their own inquiry skills. The teacher's instructional strategies framed should always move towards a more open inquiry form, where the children should be made to pose their own questions and they are also encouraged to designing their own questions for their investigations (Banchi & Bell, 2008).

Integrating Text With Inquiry Based Learning

If we are able to consider the traditional methods of science teachings that takes place in our country, then this has now been an unsuccessful reality, and we are mainly relied and heavily depended upon didactic text book based approach of teaching science. Here, it is suggested that the traditional text book based instruction are not at all an effective ways of teaching science, because the children are usually involved in limited ways and they are passive recipients of knowledge. Whereas the non-fiction, and expository text can be integrated effectively by the inquiry based instruction. The basic educational research suggest that the use of expository text should be accompanied by appropriate instructional strategies (Norris et.al., 2008). Teachers should be able to ask questions that would activate and provoke the child's prior knowledge in the subject, the child should be able to focus their attention towards learning, and we teachers should be able to invite them and guide them to make predictions before, during and after reading the expository text. These types of questions which is put forth to them would usually promote the children's comprehension of the text and this will also improve their science learning skills (Kinniburgh and Shaw, 2009).

In my opinion the structure and the designing of the text book does play a significant role and greatly affect in the science learning among the children. The main basic idea for having a text book prepared is to help the children and it should be able to supported any type of the scientific principles. These scientific principles should be explained with several examples, and these examples should serve as a cognitive support for the children. The examples so provided in the text books should be highly relevant to the main scientific ideas referred in the text book, so that the children are able to read, understand them, and they should be able to establish a proper connection between the text content and then they should be able to link them to their own personal experiences. The most important thing here is that the text book should be in a simple language, which the students are able to understand it properly.

Another important factor that needs to be understood while preparing the text book is about the diagrams. The diagrams provided in the science text book also plays a significant role in the support of the students for the understanding of the science concepts and there learning effectively, it should also be understood that a very clear diagram with the required illustration and labelled properly would help the children to represent some of the casual relationships in the text and this would also support the children to comprehension of casual mechanism.

It is also important that all the illustrations and images provided in the text books should be effectively integrated into the inquiry based method of instructions; learning by inquiry based method must also involve other skills also; such as the observation of the nature, which is also essential. It has been seen that the teachers have to face several challenges when they are trying to teach the children the science concepts live through actual observations of the nature; for instance, here are some phenomenon that are not visible during the school working hours. Let us consider the weather conditions and it is difficult for the teacher to show the skies due to the tall buildings or all trees sometimes it becomes even more frustrating especially with the young children. Similarly showing the different phases of the moon and the study of stars or showing the stars also becomes difficult. Thus, the observance of nature and teaching the children about nature would be a time consuming exercise for the teacher who wants to teach science more effectively through an inquiry approach. Under such circumstances the images provided in the text book can be used to allow the children to make observations and then they can be able to draw inference. Here the teachers may ask the children to compare their observations in nature to the illustrations and images that are provided in their text books. Sometimes, here also many science teachers may argue that the observing phenomenon of nature is important; than the use of illustrations and images in the class room, this may offer a practical and an effective way to introduce and teach science concepts among young children (Trundle & Sackes, 2008).

Early Childhood Care and Education – The Teaching Methods That can be Used Effectively

As we are all aware of the fact that the children in the early childhood years needs to be treated as soft pebbles and they are very sensitive and they need to be handled and educated carefully by the play way methods of teaching as long as they are in the foundational stage, that is between the age group from three years to six years. The best suited educational system that can be thought about for children at this age group is to educate them by play way method. Here the teachers who are being entrusted the job of teaching the children at this age group of children should be properly trained in the play way method of teaching. The play way method of teaching at this stage does have its own advantages. Here later in this book I shall be making an in depth analysis of this play way method of teaching and its effect on the children's learning.

It is a well understood fact that nearly 85% of the child's brain shows a cumulative development prior to the age of six years. This also goes to show that, this stage is a very crucial phase in the child development. It's here at this age the children needs to be properly handled and taken care of and we should be able to stimulate the child's brain right from an early growing stage, this would enable us to ensure that we are able to give the children proper good health and a proper brain development. Hence; it is essential that we are able to provide good quality education for the child right from the early childhood development, and for this we need to have a proper and an early childhood care, this needs to be achieved as soon as possible in our country. Now as per the National Policy of Education 2020, it is envisaged that we have to reach the target in our country by 2030 so that it can be assured that all the students entering in our grade I are ready and fully prepared and are strongly developed and healthy to face the school.

Early childhood care and education (ECCE) as mentioned in NCF 2023 should be an ideal and it should be flexible, multifaceted, multilevel, play based, activity based and along with the inquiry based learning which should be comprising of learning alphabets, languages, numbers, counting, understanding the colours, shapes, indoor and outdoor play, they should be able to solve puzzles and develop logical thinking, problem solving, drawing, painting and visual arts, crafts, drama and puppetry, music and movements. It is essential that we should be able to focus on the developing social capabilities, sensitivity, good behaviour, courtesy, ethics, personal and public cleanliness, team work, and cooperation. In all the basic objective of ECCE should be to attain optimal outcomes in the domain of physical and motor development capabilities the child should be able to develop a proper communication skill at an early stage and they should be good in literacy, fluent in understanding speaking and writing language, and numeracy.

It is our common observation that most of the children are engaged in the play during their early childhood years. Therefore, here the use of play becomes more significant during the early child hood years. The knowledge development by the child by way of different types of play would provide the teachers and the parents a proper foundation for the teaching strategies. Goodman (1994) was the first to report that the pre-eminent teaching for the young children can happen at the midpoint of a continuous between play and work. Hence, the professionally developed early childhood teachers who are aware of the comprehended developmental theories of play as a context are better equipped to use the play way method of the instructions and assessment. The teachers would be able to understand the importance of the play way method of teaching for the development of the child in the social, emotional, cognitive, physical, and the motor domains. Therefore, it is essential that the teachers who deal with the young children should have a strong academic background in the study of play way method and the best to evaluate problems among the children and they can offer appropriate support to the children who does have a hard time playing and these includes the normal children and the children having physical disabilities.

Play is an important element in the child's life. This play can also help the child to gain mastery on certain skills, and they would also learn to have control over their environment. Here the environment and the play are considered to be the most important element that would support each other. Though the concept of the word play seems to be simple but in reality the study of the word play is quite complex. If we have a well-planned and arranged environment, then this should enhance the child's development through learning and play. This may also help us to facilitate the class room management and it can also support the implementation of the curricular goals and objectives. The way the physical environment is designed and configured then this could influence, how the children could feel, act and behave. The physical environment should be able to allow growth and the development of the child through these activities and a material that are defined in the play areas. The room arrangement for the play activity also does play an important role in the children's social and language interactions. Whereas the poorly designed classroom could cause disruptions and negative social interactions among the children and between the children and the teacher. Now let us try to understand the play and the environment in the context of teaching and learning.

Understanding the Environment

Now, let us consider the importance of the environment in the eyes of the child and the adults. Most of the adults may feel that the environment would be an insignificant factor, but for the teachers, and the parents it is something which cannot be ignored and it is considered to be of a greater priority.

Now the physical environment may vary depending upon the age of the child and the numbers of children present in the classroom; this would also depend upon the goals of the programs that need to be achieved and the specific activities that needs to be taken up in the class room. It is also important that the child's class room is properly and well designed for various activities that needs to be undertaken in the class room, such as eating; sleeping, diapering, and it should also have some definite play areas for all the primary activity. It is in this area where most of the class room activities are performed by the children in the class room and this area is usually called as the play area. These play areas should be properly configured and properly planned so that the infants can grasp and reach to their age appropriate toys which they are able to pull it themselves when they are practicing to stand or walk. The infants will have to be placed down on the ground and they should be able to explore the environment around them with lots of toys placed around them to look at it and keep listening to things around them, feeling, chewing, pushing, pulling, stacking, rolling, turning, squeezing and shaking are the common activities seen among these children (Vance & Boals, 1989). It is essential that all the play activities should be held in the same or in one room and sometimes the children are seen to fall asleep while playing, the children need to be supervised properly and the sleep areas as far as possible should be separate may be in the same room and we should also make sure that the children's sleep patterns are not disturbed under any circumstances. We should be assured that we are able to provide a warm, cozy and a home like environment in the class room then this would provide the infants with a healthy social and an emotional environment.

The physical environment for a toddler class room should have the following area and they are an eating, napping, diapering, toileting and play areas. Here also at this stage the play continues to be a very important factor and learning centers at this stage thus becomes more obvious and important for this age group. At this stage the areas are to be sub divide into the following areas such as dramatics block, art, library, manipulative and science learning centers. The toddlers need space that would allow them to go around and explore and carry out experiments and discover things around their own surrounding environment. The toddlers are seen constantly moving or they are always on the go and they need many opportunities to practice newly emerging skills (Vartuli, 1987).

The preschool children's class room will be the similar to that of the toddler class room, but the only difference here would be the diapering area, which is no longer required in the preschool class room. However, they have the following areas and they are the eating, napping, toileting and play areas continue to be essential. The learning centers are emphasized in the preschool class room; and such centers would include dramatic block, art, library, dress-up, music, and science and so on.

What Are Learning Centers?

In the earlier paragraphs we had been talking about the term Learning centers, now let us try to understand what are these learning centers? These learning centers can also be referred to as learning areas; they are the type of system that is mainly used to arrange a class room or organic materials in a class room. The term learning center is an important center because it is associated where the learning takes place only in these specific centers (Brewer, 2004). The most important fact is that the learning occurs every day and everywhere whether it is in the class room or outside the class room. The learning center can be defined in this text also as a specific location or area where instructional materials are placed and organized in a class room. Some of the common learning areas that are seen in the early childhood class room are art, library, listening, writing activities, blocks, dramatics, play, science, discovery activities and manipulative mathematical/games. All these areas will be needed to be considered as per the children's ages, their interests, and abilities and these needs to be changed accordingly.

Equipment's and Materials Required for an Early Childhood Classroom Teaching

Teaching in the early childhood class room is not an easy task. This requires a lot of effort planning and a proper materials required in the class room setup. Here in this part we will try to understand the materials required in the early childhood class room teaching. However; before we proceed with the materials and the equipment's required for the early childhood class room teaching, let us look into what are the physical environment required for the children learning by the play way method. The children will have to be provided with a very well arranged environment which would enhance the child's growth and development through the process of learning by the play way method.

This should also be helpful in the proper management of the class room teaching and will also support the implementation of all the curricular goals and its objectives (Catron & Allen, 2007). It is also important that the physical environment provided to the child should be properly designed and configured in such a way that we should be able to influence the child's feelings, act and their behaviour. The physical environment thus provided should be able to allow the growth and development of the child through their activities and the materials provided should be definitely arranged in the play areas.

We should be aware of the fact that the room arrangement for the play way activity is almost very important and this may also play a prominent role in the child's development of the social and the language interaction. For instance; if we are having the reading and the writing centers very close to the music area then this would usually cause disruption among the children, because those children who is trying to concentrate and practice on these skills of writing and reading.

Then, these children may get frustrated when they do not have an organized environment to concentrate and study for themselves. In short, I have to say that the arrangements of the physical environment would be the direct image of the teachers planning and this will also help in the children learning.

Whenever; we are planning a play way class room then, one thing that we need to bear in mind is that about the physical environment should vary depending upon the age and the number of the children in the class room. The planning of the physical environment may also depend upon the goals of the program that has to be taught and also the specific activities that needs to be performed in the class room. Therefore; the class room for the infants should have sufficient space for their eating, sleeping, diapering the play areas which is mainly for the primary activities. Most of the activities for the children are carried out are always in the play areas, the play areas for the infants should be properly configured, planned and arranged, so that the infants are able to move around and grasp and the infants are able to reach an age appropriate toys, pull themselves up and play by picking up from the area where it is stacked, when they are practicing to stand up and walking. Most of the infants should be kept on the floor, so that they are able to explore their own environment with the available toys for which they look at it and listening to things occurring around them, feeling them, chewing, pushing, pulling, stacking, rolling, turning, squeezing, and shaking are some of the activities the infants are seen doing in their class area (Vance & Boals, 1989).

As we know that the learning areas are also known as the learning centers; these are some of the vital systems used in arranging the class room or organize the materials required in a class room. The term learning center has been judged by many because it has a connotation that learning takes place only in these specific centers (Brewer, 2004). The learning occurs every day and everywhere in the learning center, whether it is in the class room or outside the class room. In the early childhood class room some of the learning areas that are most common are the class room library, art area, listening and writing activities area or blocks, dramatics play, Science/discovery activities, and manipulative/mathematics/ games area. Keeping all these matter in mind we will have to consider the class room keeping in mind the child's age, their interest and abilities and thus accordingly we will have to make changes in the class room.

The play materials that are provided in the class room should be selected properly and are extremely essential for the multiple developmental perspective of each child, such as for the cognitive, social, emotional, physical development, and for the development of language. The teachers should be able to provide cognizance of the age appropriate play materials/equipment's and the furniture required for the class room teaching. Some of the common beneficial play materials required in the class room of the at the pre - school and the primary grade schools that are required by the teachers are also listed here below:

Some of the manipulative/games are

Some of the equipment's required for the manipulative games are the soft toys of all animals, hand puppets, some simple puzzles, beads and strings, sewing cards, manipulative materials ranging from stacking rings to very complex materials, tinker toys, LEGO bricks, Bristle blocks,

Some of the materials required for the teaching of Science

The following materials are required for the teaching of science in the class room and they are as follows; Aquarium, terrarium, magnets of various kinds, magnifying glasses, glass slabs, glass Prism, metric measuring equipment's, test tubes, slides, Petri dishes, capillary tubes, blocks of various patterns, pegs and the peg boards, scales, rhythm instruments, sand box, water table with tap, work bench with equipment's, Alphabetic blocks in English and in Hindi, similar blocks of numbers, solid blocks of cylinder, sphere, hexagonal, circle, square, rectangle.

Materials required for Physical Education

Beam balance, tumbling mat, steps made of plastic, ladder, rocking boat, walking board, jungle gym, fabric tunnel, sawhorses, climbing ladder, climbing rope, balls of various types, ropes, hula hoops, bowling set, rocking horse, rocking chair, outdoor equipment mainly required for gardening, indoor games such as chess, carom board, and so on.

Providing Safe Environment – its Advantages

Several studies carried out in this direction have indicated that the way the class rooms are to be arranged and the way it looks should be significant because this would influence the children and the adult's behavior. So whenever we are setting a class room for the early childhood education then we should be able to consider the following points:

1. The learning center should be planned well as a multiple user class; it should not be for just one specific center or for a topic.

2. We have to make sure that the learning center should have sufficient natural light in the class room. This natural light would reduce the use of electrical energy and the most important factor is that this would enhance the children ability in task performance and this will also improve the appearance of the area.

3. When planning always try to keep the noisy and the quite areas separate. The noisy areas such as the dramatic, play and the music area should be located at one end of the room, opposite to the quite area; this would allow each area to have its activities in a comfortable location.

A safe environment would always encourage exploration and play behavior among the children. A safe environment is very important for teachers teaching young children and teachers working in the child care centers. When the parents bring the children to the child care center, they may expect for the child's safety. It is assumed that the playground, equipment's, toys and other materials should be safe for the child to use and the teacher would carefully supervise the children's activities.

The teachers should be able to prevent the children from injuries and age related confrontations, make sure that the infants and the toddlers are expected to have a separate play area from the preschool children. A large open space is expected without any obstacles for the play area is encouraged for very young children. This type of environment would help the children to move along and explore their environment without any type of hesitation.

Fire safety regulations

This is one of the most important factors which is required to be considered in all the schools. The fire regulators mainly required are the fire extinguishers, as well as the smoke and carbon monoxide detectors, this should be present in the class room and they should be in a good working condition in all the class rooms. The fire exit, fire alarm, and the fire escape route should be properly marked designated and properly labeled very clearly and should be visible. The teachers should be very familiar with the exit routes, and the location of the building. The teachers should be well trained with the fire safety procedures by way of fire safety drills. The teachers should be able to operate the fire extinguishers when in case of emergency. This would help the children to face the emergency situation without any fear.

Sanitation and bathroom Facilities

It is very important that the class room toys and the class room furniture should be properly sanitized on a daily basis as this would reduce the spread of germs. The child care center should have the required number of sinks, toilets, soap dispensers, towel rack, etc. so that the children can make use of it regularly. The bathroom facilities should be accessible in both indoor and outdoor play area. The bathrooms should be established as per the health regulations required that is one toilet and one sink for every 10 -12 students in the school.

Lighting, ventilation, and Temperature

The presence of adequate light in the class room is an essential factor, the most important and desirable light is the natural light coming from the windows or from the glass doors. However, if this is not available then the non –glare light would also be essential. It is always better if all the rooms are covered with blind folds to control the light and it should have the locks. All the rooms should have appropriate air ventilators fans, air conditioners etc. and should be provided with heating device in colder area for a comfortable class room environment.

Understanding the Play and its Importance

The word play is a term which is regularly use in our daily life, but it is difficult to define the word play. Many teachers, educators and the philosophers have defined the term play with some variation to its meaning. The broad category of activities that are covered by the term play include, a greater variety of behaviour, such as swinging, sliding, running, digging in the dirt, building with blocks, dancing to music, making up nonsense rhyming words, dressing up, and pretending and so on. Because of these many varieties in activities, so, no one could define the word play adequately.

If we take the opinion of most of the scientists and educationalist, they argue that the word play need not be defined, but all the studies have revealed that the word play is the opposite of work and it is mostly done during the vacation or weekends or with or in the presence of the children. At the same time, understanding the play on an academic point of view is critically important for the early child hood teachers. Some of the researchers have tried to define the definition of the term play by means of research and the most suggested definition of the word play is as stated below:

Now when a man plays he must intermingle with objects or things and the people around him in a similarly uninvolved and in a light fashion. He must do something which he has chosen to do without being compelled by urgent interest or by strong passion. He must feel entertained and free of any fear or hope of serious consequences. He is on vacation from social and economic reality – or as in most commonly emphasized that he is not at work.

Based on the above context Bruner (1972), came up with the psychological definition of play which is as followed:

Play appears to serve several centrally important functions. First, it is the means of minimizing the consequences of one's actions and of learning, therefore it is a less risky situation, second, the play should provide an excellent opportunity to try combinations of behaviour that would, under functional pressure, never be tried.

According to Bruner, play can be seen as the main opportunity for children to take risks without fear of failure. His definition also proposes that creativity and play activities are closely related. That is, if the children explore and experiment in their play, the possibilities for creative outcomes are greatly enhanced without the fear of failure.

Looking in to these factors, I would sum up and put play as an act performed by the adult without fear and that gives mental satisfaction and delight. This would provide all type mental fatigue what we the adults have.

Vygotsky offered additional insight into the childhood play. According to him, imaginative play is the main focus for the general development of the child. He further suggested that we must challenge the child to increase his higher levels of imaginative skills and functioning, what he referred to as the zone of proximal development.

The Developmental Characteristics of the Play

We all know that the play is an activity which is an important activity and several studies have been carried out, and of which the contributions of Piaget's and Vygotsky's is one which is important for the understanding of play activity in the dimensions related to the abstract thinking, imagination and for the creation of rules among the children. Piaget (1952) saw play as an important phenomenon or an agent for the construction of knowledge within the individual child by interacting with the objects and it may also be with the toys or any other objects or with their own peers. On the other hand, studies carried out by Vygotsky (1978) shows that the play, also plays an important role in social interaction and it is also believed that the children would learn about self, through their interactions with others. Ultimately, it is through these act of play, that most of the children would come to see the development of self. Studies made by Mead (1934) found that play to be a major vehicle for the young children to learn how to differentiate their own perspectives from those of others children.

The Play and the Cognitive Development

We know that the play activity does have a significant role to play in the cognitive development of the child. Now to understand, how the play would function and help in the development of a complex and an adaptive system, as the children grow older, it is also helpful for us to review some of the commonly visible and recognized forms and the developmental sequences seen with the play. Sara Smilancky (1990) has provided models presenting five basic forms of play and they are stated as below:

1. *Functional Play or exploratory play*

   The functional or exploratory play is a sensorimotor approach in which a child learns about the nature of his or her surroundings. Here the examples mainly include dumping, filling, staking, water play and other outdoor activities as play.

2. *The Constructive Play*

   The constructive play is a type, which describes the children were they try in combining pieces or entities, such as for constructing something with blocks. The purpose of this type of play is to make the children construct something and/or work out some problem.

3. *Dramatic play entails pretending*

   This is a play in which the child pretends themselves to be someone else, for example sometimes we see that the child could be seen to act as a teacher or a doctor or as fireman. Or a police man. This type of play does not require any type of social interaction with other children.

4. *Sociodramatic play*

   This is a form of dramatic play in which more than one player interacting around a particular theme and at a time trajectory over in which the play continues and evolves. The children try to enact as real life type of play activities. The best type of play which is commonly seen among the Indian children are the thief (chor) and the police.

5. *Games with rules*

This type of game mainly encompasses cooperative play, which will often end determining who is the winners and the losers. These games are distinguished by child – controlled rules and thus are different from the competitive games usually called "sports". Children begin the games with rules at about the age of 6. Games with rules become more evident as children move from early middle childhood. This type of play behaviour suggests that the children are able to understand the social rules of our culture.

Associated Social Development and the Play

Number of studies were carried out to understand and describe the children's social play. It was Mildred Parten (1933) who presented a model of socialization of skills in play, which is considered as one of the best in this field. He stated that the children would engage themselves in the solitary play until the age of 2½ years. Gradually later the children are moved from the solitary play to parallel play, later they would move to associated play and then lately they are seen to the cooperative play. The different types of plays as mentioned by Mildred Parten are mentioned here below:

1. ***Solitary Play***

   Many a times we might have seen the children playing alone, this may be a bit usually with the toys that are different from those of the other children playing nearby. Most of the children at this stage make no attempt to get closer to or interact with other children. This gives a very clear indication that the level of social interaction seen among the children at this stage is very low. Here it is important and it could be realize that there is a lack of social values among the children. However, the solitary play should be encouraged as a part of a young child's activities. It is understood that those children who have learned to be comfortable in solitary play are more likely to succeed in working independently.

2. ***Parallel play***

   This is usually seen among the children from the age group between 2 ½ to 3 ½ years old were they continue to play independently, but gradually now at this stage they are among their peers and they will be using the toys that are similar to those of the other children around them. It's just as parallel lines run side by side, children in this stage also play beside each other, but not with others. There is an awareness among the children nearby but they do have very little interaction.

3. *Associative play*

It can be seen that as the children gets mature, it has been seen that they begin to engage themselves in an associative play, this begins at an age around about 3 ½ years old. In this type of play, it can be seen that the children truly play with others. Here it can be observed that the children would loan and borrow toys or lay materials among themselves. At this stage it can also be seen that the associations are more important than the play activity itself. The children begin to form smaller play groups and spend considerable time moving from one activity to the next activity with their playmates remaining together.

4. *Cooperative play*

This is an event that is seen to occurs at the age above 4 ½ years of age. This stage has been said to be the final type of social beginning. This is the highest level of social play seen; it can be characterized by the children playing in the groups as they did in associative play, but now at this stage the children are seen to demonstrate division of labor, whether working on a group project they are seen to cooperate to attain a common goal. This can be also considered as a more sophisticated type of play because it requires the presence of negotiation among two or more children.

Other Developmental Characters of Play

1. Emotional Development and Play

The play is considered to be one of the most excellent vehicle which would provide the children to have a proper emotional development (Johnson; Christie and Yawkey, 1999). It is from here were the children are able to master their various emotional issues such as anxiety, frustration, normal developmental conflicts, traumatic situations, unfamiliar concepts, and an overwhelming experiences in their play. This means that, it is during the play that would help the children to find new ways of dealing with their own emotions and their reality. Now as the children starts playing, then they are able to develop and explore themselves all the properties of various things that is occurring around them and they are also able to find the extract information about the environment around them. They are also able to imitate, recreate and rehearse their roles and this would also help the children to understand and solve their own problems related to everyday living. The children shall also form the relationship, and they would share their feelings, cooperate, and master their feelings, they will also extend the range of their experiences, test ideas, and form associations between the things, events, and concepts. The other major emotional benefit of play is that it gives the children numerous opportunities to feel to be good about themselves. As there is no right or wrong way to play, the children here have multiple experiences in play, this would have a positive influence about the concepts of the child.

2. Development of Language through Play

It has been observed that the act of play does have a major influence on the children learning the language and not only that the children are able to master and develop the skills of communication. It is observed that when the children are seen to play then they are seen using the language to interact with their peers, and as they interact they are seen using different tones and sounds to regulate their speech, in this process they are gradually able to develop and master their vocabulary. It is also further understood that the play and the language developed by the child would promotes them to develop their own experience, this activity also tones up their perception of the rules underlying the use of voice or conversation patterns of the language (Bergen, 2002). The children as they grow, they are also able to improve their oral and written language skills. The languages used during the play would also encourage them to develop the meta-linguistic awareness – their ability to reflect consciously on the linguistic operations and analytical orientations of language which also help and generate the literacy development. This meta-linguistic awareness would also allow the children to think about the words which they will be using in their conversations. The children's experiences with words and their ability to manipulate their use, meaning, and grammar. Through these words, the child would experiment them with rhythm, sound, and forms (Johnson, 1928). Garney (1990) proposed that every characteristics of the language can be better understood through play.

3. Physical Development and Play

Physical development is one of the most important and greatest characteristics of the play. Here the play has been an activity which may be through dancing, jumping, throwing, running and generally moving around and so on. Here the children are seen often moving around and strengthening their gross motor muscle development through the use of their own large muscles activities, (Gallahue, 1982) and the other types of play activity areas are such as cutting, eating, writing, buttoning, painting and dressing, provided for their fine motor development or refinements for the skills that requires the use of smaller muscles. It is through the play that the children are naturally able to use and learn to refine their gross and fine motor skills and their coordination. Now, as the children gets older they are able to use their muscles continually in some or more in many complex ways, integrating larger and fine muscle movements with their visual perception (Henniger, 2008).

4. Creativity and Play

Creativity is one of the most important characteristic which a child has to develop and this play activity does play an important role to development of creativity. It is through this creativity the children are able to use their imagination to invent or produce or create something new. At the early years, it is very important that we encourage the children for the development of creativity; the children need to be provoked to develop this skill. The young children should be promoted and should be provided much opportunity to express and question, so they are able to come up with their own idea and develop their own creative talents. For example, during free play, the young children experiment with the available things and they apply their ideas and create new combinations that they might have never experienced before. As per the observations of Wasserman (1992) states that; "The creation of new ideas does not come from minds trained to follow doggedly what is already known; the creation comes from tinkering and playing with things around them, from which new forms of idea emerge". The Children are able to develop their own creativity through play situations that requires them to use their own imagination (Singer, 1973). Therefore, play materials are supposed to help them elicit new ideas for children and this help fostering creativity among the children this helps them to promote a healthy development and a happy disposition.

5. Developmental Benefits of Play

It can be understood that the play provides a joyful experience for the children, and it could open up a new world for these children. Every early childhood teacher who is teaching these children does have a desire to provide purposeful play opportunities for these children that would enhance their development and this may lead to learning, we must never forget that one of the greatest gifts of childhood is their ability to pursue things seemingly in an insignificant manner with interests and make them to explore tiny details to one's heart's content. Play is no doubt a marvelous activity; it's a renewable resource in the life of a child. Play can follow any path of the child's desire and this will end when the child decides to move on to something else or when the demands of living in the world intrude on the child's own agenda. Play is practical, authentic, and it is often suggested that the educational endeavor for young children who are gaining much of their knowledge about the world around them through their senses. Young children are very much dependent on this sensory learning and physical contact with their environment (Catron & Allen, 2007). When play is sense based, it could encourage children's active and their involvement and this is relevant and meaningful to them since they find it easier to attend and remain interested. When children are active in their play, then learning becomes much easier.

Use of Play by Teachers for Children Learning and Development

Teachers are the persons who would be able to help the children to learn things through the process of play, this can be done by proper planning and organizing learning areas. It is a well-known fact; that the learning areas mainly assist the children in the development of the socio-emotional, cognitive, and physical growth of the child. Learning areas mainly provide the children with an opportunity to explore and experience the feelings and the cognitive tasks while using their motor skills that are crucial in their later part in their life (Shipley, 2007). There are specific procedures that have to be followed during the early childhood education and they are as under:

1. The children should have the freedom to choose their own play experiences.

2. The children should be provided with an environment which would offer play alternatives that would be meaningful and accessible to all the children.

3. The play experiences provided to the children should be mainly based up on the objectives derived from the observations of the children, in order to facilitate their developmental progress from their present level to a higher level of development.

4. The teachers should be able to plan a range of play experiences from the simple to the complex and they shall begin with very concrete learning challenges in which the concepts or skills are to be mastered by the child and they are made clear to the child and it should be observable to the learner.

5. The teachers should be able to provide a proper balance of the structured and open- ended activities.

6. The teachers should be able to provide or maintain a proper balance of individuals and group activities so as to allow the children's unique style of learning.

7. It is essential that the required equipment's, materials, and the supplies should be placed in a well-defined learning centers that would ensure children's receipt of the messages from their environment about what they should be doing and learning in each learning centers.

Source: Adapted from Shipley, D. (2007).

Whenever we are planning the creation of a learning centers in the schools, then the teachers should be able to consider the following steps also:

1. They will have to determine the developmental goals and objectives.

2. It is important to understand and know the principles of learning and children's learning styles.

3. The teachers will have to plan well before designing and setting up the learning centers.

4. and finally, the teachers should be able to evaluate the learning environment.

Adapting Play to Individual Learners

By now we should be aware about the importance of play, and this is responsible for the various development of the children, this would also foster the children's development. These ideas are not different from those children who are having disabilities. More children with disabilities will have to be access to the main stream of class room development due to the mandated inclusion of educational policies and the implementation of less restrictive environments, so there are chances that teachers will have the child in their classroom with special needs. When such children with disabilities enter the classroom, then the teacher should be aware of that and these children might require more time, for instruction, or may require additional help which needs to be provided in the classroom. It is important and would be helpful for the teacher to be well informed about the specific disability of a child and how we can adapt play activities appropriately.

There are children who really have difficulty with learning, memory, or problem solving ability, such children can gain a great deal through the practice of play, here I would like to refer to the Bollywood film "Tare Zamen pe" here the film depicts the way the teacher teaches the child by play way methods and achieves his goal in educating the child with learning disabilities. For instance, if a teacher facilitates the right opportunities, to these children then they can benefit from such activities such as classifying, identifying, sorting, matching, problem solving, seriating, number concepts, and spatial concepts. Similarly, children with communication problems can also become more skilled at by using signs in their play, and they can improve their ability to communicate in an increasingly complex way.

Play enhances the developmental process by providing situations to practice symbols that would result in language improvement. For example, the symbolic play is important for later development because it is an indicator of the development of representational thought, which will help to stimulate the children's language and their comprehension skills.

The idea which we have is that the "children learn through play" has directed by the early childhood teachers for decades. This simple phrase provides the rationale for several models of early childhood programs and different theoretical approaches. It has also become a way of explaining almost anything that a professional early childhood teacher does to keep his or her children occupied in the classroom. The emphasis on learning through the play way method will continue. The fact is that the children are active learners who construct their own knowledge and understanding of the world around them through play way experiences has these become a cornerstone of professional early childhood teachers. As a professional educator or teacher, you must be increasingly ready to give children more of the responsibility for their own learning.

Finally, the role of the teacher teaching children in the early childhood education plays a very good foundation for the building of a young talented and a responsible citizen of this great country. So the role of the teacher teaching in the early childhood education is eminent.

❖126❖

CHAPTER 4

Teaching by Play Way Method at Pre-Primary and the Primary Level

In the previous chapters we have come across the term play way method of teaching again and again. It is also understood that the word play, is also considered as an important activity, and it is through these the children are able to acquire knowledge and they are also able to understand in a better way about their own surroundings and the environment. Now here let us try to understand, what is play way method of teaching. This play way method of teaching not only focuses on the subjective development among the children, but it also helps in the emotional development of the child. In this method of learning by playing act is the only driving force and I believe that the entire learning method revolves around this activity – based learning. We are also being able to understand that this activity based learning also encourages expression and creativity skills among the children.

The play way method of teaching in education was first introduced by a German scholar and an educator Fredrich Froebel (1782 – 1852). He also developed the concept of Kindergarten. The main objective of Froebel work was to introduce the spirit of play in the educational institutions.

He also believed and advocated that the best way for the children to learn was through the medium of guided play in a friendly natural environment.

It is a known fact that the children do have a God gifted ability of imitating the adults during their play, and it is during this playing in which the children are able to learn a lot about the ways of the world around them. It is this concept which was incorporated to introduce play to educate the young children, this was the best way to utilize their natural abilities and teach them the required skills based on their habits. Froebel also believed that the mothers and the Kindergarten teachers can use this technique carefully to educate about the child's nature, inclination and the stages of development. Today it has become mandatory for the aspiring pre and primary teachers and the Montessori teachers to internalize the importance of educating the very young students by following the play way principles.

Why Play Way Method?

These many days the preprimary stage of education was often overlooked, but this stage is the one which actually needs immense exploration and more attention. The reason behind this was because the base of the child's education is formed right from the preprimary school education; and at this stage the play way method of education is a very popular methodology for imparting knowledge to the children and the same is now introduced in all the major parts of our country in the preschool education. It's also known that while going to the play school the children first step out of their home. Hence an environment of play is entertained for them in the preprimary school, this will provide them the feeling of comfort and this would also help them to create a bond between the teacher and the child. It is also found that the children always tend to get excited if we are able to add certain fun element and play is involved in it. It is with this play way method, the children would be able to give wings to their imagination, they will also be able to make improvement in their various skills like motor, creative, imagination, aesthetic, cognitive and linguistic and so on.

The play way method is one of the unique method of learning for a child, and this can be customized as per the child's interest and their requirements. This may vary from child to child. Here the teacher will have to plan, workout and develop a different customized learning activities by creating a joyful environment and teacher shall plan the activities ranging from simple to complex, depending upon the teachers, who would decide the best for child other than to get a complete feeling of freedom. This method of learning is unplanned and hence encourages the complete freedom of expression. The common traditional methods of assessing the children would be based on the grading system which are completely eliminated under this method. Here the teacher will assess the aptitudes and the skills of a child on regular basis at regular intervals and the children parents are informed at regular intervals. Based on the children performance they are promoted to the next level or to the next class by participating in ample of various activities like the music, communication with the teachers and other kids, art, learning and inculcating various skills etc. all these activities ensures the child's development such as physical, intellectual, psychological along with the developmental different skills.

There is no rigid method for the application of the play way method of learning and the same can be combined with any other methods of learning also. All the appropriate knowledge regarding this method can be acquired by preschool trainer certification. The school who wishes to incorporate or introduce the play way method of learning in its curriculum needs to study the minute details of it and prepare the setup accordingly.

Principles of Play Way Method

- It is understood that we should have a practical approach and this would help learaning for the child.

- It is also essential that we are able to provide a complete atmosphere of freedom which is conducive for learning.

- It is also encouraged that the learning methods used should be of real life situations.

- These methods provides a plethora of opportunities for the child to express themselves.

Why Use Play Way Method?

➢ The use of play way method would turn the entire learning into fun elements by involving the factor of play in it.

➢ The use of play way method develops a feeling of satisfaction among the children.

➢ By this play way method every child is given equal exposure and ample of opportunities for learning and participation.

➢ By using this method, the child will acquire and inculcated various skills along with the required knowledge.

➢ This method would also help the child to get connected with their peers and the teachers easily.

➢ By using this method, we can expect to facilitate and create an overall and holistic development of the child.

The school education of the twenty-first century should be greatly indebted to the educational philosophers, pioneer educationist like Froebel and his mentor Pestalozzi for steering away for imparting education from being a tutor centric activity education to a learner centric one. As a result of all these, the present day nursery teachers training programme now train the following; the principles of the play way method. It is also seen that the teacher training institutes that offer Montessori course or preprimary teachers training course have also introduced the play way method in their course curriculum.

Significance of Play Way Method in Child's Education

By now we must have understood that the main essence of childhood is to have an endless opportunity to play. The child is the happiest when they are engrossed in play, and this play can happen in any form, such as; imitation by the child of any of the family members, or playing with toys, or playing tag, hide and seek, or simply running here and there in small groups. This play would help the children to improve their motor skills, enhance their power of imagination and also inculcate creativity in them. Froebel, Madam Montessori all realized that the use of play does have a means of educating children.

The Montessori course also advocates that the method of educating children through various activities would keep the children engaged creatively and they are engaged in a learning conducive happy environment. Today all the nursery school teachers training institute as well as the pre and primary teachers training courses now a day's train its candidates into the Montessori method of teaching also.

Play Way Methods

The word play was defined by Froebel and as per his view - "Play is considered as the purest most spiritual activity of man, at this stage and at the same time, typical of human life as a whole of the inner hidden natural life in man all things. It gives, therefore joy contentment, inner and outer rest, peace with the world. It holds the source of all that is good".

Play is an innate, creative, joyful, non-serious, interesting and recreated activity. It is the activity in which the natural urge of the child finds a spontaneous expression. It is regarded as the language of the child, which the child cannot express through the language, but here the child is able to express that through his behaviour and through that behaviour is the play.

According to Froebel, "education is a development from which man's life broadens until it has related itself to nature, until it enters sympathetically into all activities of the society, until its processes of unfolding child's innate powers and to awaken his spiritual nature which may enable the child to realize his inner unity, achievements of race and aspiration of humanity. He clearly emphasized on natural release of the child's physical and mental powers through which the child will develop a balanced personality". He as further said, "Play is the highest phase of the child's development and the source of all that is good". All the educationist made efforts in order to bring play into the field of education. The play way method was first used as a method of teaching by Cadwell Cook. This was first used for teaching the different plays of Shakespeare's by Cook. Here he noticed that they took more interest in those plays where they themselves were involved in the activity. He said, "Good work is more often the result of spontaneous effort and free interest than of compulsion and forced application. Effectiveness of learning lies not in reading and listening, but in action, performance and experience". He further said, "the core of my faith is that only work worth doing in play; buy play He means doing anything with one's heart in it. Only that child learns best who learns with interest and with a purpose and sees significance in what he does".

Principles of Playway Methods

Some of the basic principles of the play way methods is mentioned here below:

i. Learning by Doing.

ii. Principles of individual differences.

iii. Sympathetic attitude.

i. Learning by doing:

Every human being and the child also have five senses, and they are as follows

a) Sense of vision

b) Sense of smell

c) Sense of hearing

d) Sense of taste

e) Sense of touch

It is the training of these five senses, that helps in making the child in the all-round development of an individual. The principles of learning by doing mainly involves the maximum usage of their senses. Any kind of knowledge which the child gains from his head and hands becomes interesting and purposeful for the child. the children's experiments and the discovery made by themselves, the required knowledge gained by the child by means of play way method.

ii. Principles of individual differences:

The play way method takes into account the individual differences of the learner. Every individual works according to his differences in different spheres like their interests, attitudes, sentiments, capabilities, intelligence level etc. it makes the learning easy and understandable by involving every learner according to their difference.

ii. Sympathetic Attitude:

The play way method develops a congenial environment in the teaching learning processes. It does not create an artificial environment or any compulsion on the learners, everyone is free to do and act according to his own interests. Whenever, children need suggestions they should accept them without any hesitation.

Differences Between Work and Play

Work and play are the two entities of the same coin. What is "work" for one person may be a play for another. For example, maintaining a garden is the work of a gardener for his livelihood; whereas the same work of gardening would become a hobby for a house wife to relieve her mental stress. Basically both the activities remain the same. The work is the same for the gardener and the house wife.

Characteristics of Work

The work is considered as difficult. It is being thrust by others.

The physical work brings lot of tiredness.

More concentration on work would make us tired. It can be controlled.

Characteristics of Play

Play in any form would give pleasure. Voluntary acceptance with involvement.

Physical work turns into an enjoyable experiment. More concentration towards play but no tiredness. There is more freedom during play.

The play acts as a stimulant which consist of pleasure and satisfaction to the basic play.

The Role of Teachers in Play Way Method

Till the early twenty first century, the kindergarten teachers continued to emphasized the ideas of Froebel for developing the social side of the child's nature and to create a sense of readiness for learning. One of the most important outcome that needs to be developed for the kindergarten child is their readiness for the intellectual learning, that would come later in his educational career. It is the creative skills of the teacher which would help them to develop new learning activities and various learning devices which will help the teacher to have a proper and feasible class room climate. The learning environment which is developed by the teacher must make the children feel that the learning materials are to be prepared after proper planning and designing the learning activities.

The learning activities are to be arranged properly right from the simple concepts to the complex. During the learning process the teacher must be a guide, supervisor and a leader for the learner. Evaluation of the children must also be achieved through various play way activities. Evaluation should not be ignored. Playing is one of the predominant factor, in this method, if this act rejuvenates the children and helps them in their learning, then it would also enhance their learning abilities. Therefore, it becomes the duty of a talented teacher to make use of the best aspects of this play way method in the highest level of teaching and learning.

Procedural Details in Play Way Method

As we are aware of the fact that when we were children, we also loved to play, so are the children, they also love to play and play is their basic and natural instinct. It is due to this reason the play way method in teaching and learning was conceived by Friedrich Wilhelm August Froebel, who is also referred as the father of the Kindergarten method. Froebel referred "play" as work of the children. It is considered as the purest, most spiritual and an important product of man at this stage.

There is a theory, which states that a child understands his needs and goals while the child is at playing. So, it is very important to teach the children with the play way method. It has been proved beyond doubt that the maximum amount of learning results while the child is playing games. When the child is playing games then the environment is very much relaxed, and this makes learning interesting and funny. I feel that, this is the most desirable method of learning for kids. The informal and a free atmosphere is given to the kids then the chance to learn new concepts, idea, math's and even language is possible. Toys can sometimes be the root of mathematical toys which help the children to learn math's and some apparatus like the checkers boards, magic square, puzzles and building blocks are also used to make teaching and learning an effective and a memorable experience for the learner.

It has been seen that the innovations made by Kindergarten uses extraordinary visual materials to reconstruct this successful system to teach young children about art, design, mathematics and the nature. Fredrich Froebel's ideas does provide the major direction for kindergarten curriculum during the last half of the nineteenth century. Many of his ideas can still be observed in many of the kindergarten today. Learning through play, group games, goal oriented activities, and outdoor time are some of the major activities seen in most of the Kindergarten. However, the theories on "Spiritual Mechanism", as well as some others have been forgotten or discredited, but his role as the developer of kindergarten is still remembered.

Froebel developed a series of gifts and occupation for use in kindergarten. Representing what Froebel identified as fundamental forms, the gifts made by him had both their actual physical appearance and also a hidden symbolic meaning. They were mainly to stimulate the child to bring in them the fundamental concepts that they need to represented their mental consciousness. Some of the Froebel's gifts were of the following items: -

- Six soft colored balls.

- A wooden sphere, cube and the cylinder.

- A large cube divided into eight smaller cubes.

- A large cube divided into eight oblong blocks.

- A large cube divided into twenty-one whole, six halves, and twelve quarter cubes.

- A large cube divided into eighteen whole oblongs, three divided length wise, three divided breadthwise.

- Quadrangular and triangular tablets used for arranging figures.

- Sticker for outlining figures.

- Whole and half wire rings for outlining figures.

- Various materials required for drawing, perforating, embroidering, paper cutting, weaving or braiding, paper folding, modelling and interlacing.

As a series, the gifts began with the simple undifferentiated sphere or circle and moved to more complex objects. Following the idealistic principles of synthesis of opposites, Froebel's cylinders represented the integration of the sphere and the cube. The various cubes and their subdivisions were the building blocks that children could use to create geometrical and architectural designs. Using the sticks and rings to trace designs on paper, children exercised the hand's small muscles, coordinated their hand and eye movements, and took the first steps towards drawing and later they start writing. The occupations were items such as paper, pencils, wood, sand, clay, straw, and sticks for use in constructive activities. Kindergarten activities included games, songs, and stories designed to assist in sensory and physical development and socialization.

Play Way Method in Teaching – Here Are Some Practical Ways

In play, a child would experience the pleasure of performing a task for its own sake, whenever enjoyment is introduced as an activity, it is said to be done in the "play way" spirit. The play way method may make things difficult and a boring task, it may be delightful and pleasurable to the doer that means the children, but this does not mean shirking away from real work; it is nothing but introducing elements of happiness and satisfaction otherwise it may be dull, boring and an irksome task.

A class room of the young children are mostly vibrant and has full of life. The children really enjoy learning through several ways. The activities in the play way method are according to the child's ability and physical fitness of the child in which the spirit of play may be utilized in the work of the teaching of mother tongue or any languages, by talking, listening, using toys, working with material, painting and drawing, singing, dancing, running and jumping. As a teacher we will have to use all these ways to work with our children.

1. Conversations

As we are all aware of the fact that the language is the medium through which children talk to themselves and to others, it is through this the children are able to construct sentences and get themselves to get a grip on their reality, it is this language through which the child is able to understand and use the language clearly and cogently is very essential for learning. So conversations are very important for the children to get connected with the peers and the people and it is through them they connect to all the things around them. If we the teachers are able to converse with our children in the class room, then this would help us to build a very good relationship of trust with the children. The conversations in the class room can be divided into two kinds.

i. Free Conversations

In this type of conversations, the teacher gathers some children around him and allow them to talk about all the interesting things that have occurred during the day, on their way to school or any other information which the children needs to share. The main objective of the teacher is to question the children and gather more information which they wish to talk about their own experiences.

ii. Structured Conversations

These are the planned conversations which are properly organized by the teachers. This is a common activity that occur in the morning assembly where the children come together and talk and think through the topic provided to them together. Here the topics are often about the children's daily events and happenings.

Whenever a specific topic is chosen, then there is a focus which will help the children's language information and understanding of that topic.

Questions with yes or no answers are not very helpful at this time. Questions that push children to speak, and describe something using more words and sentences are useful. The small children should never be reprimanded for giving wrong answers. All the children should be getting equal opportunities to participate and to express themselves without being judged.

2. Storytelling

All the children are found of the stories, the stories are really fascinating, beautiful, enchanting and listening to stories are really a great fun for the young children.

They love to listen to the stories which is told with feeling, with gesture and animated expressions are magical and take your breath away.

Stories are a good medium for learning about social relationships, ethical choices, for understanding and experiencing emotions, and becoming aware of life skills. While listening the stories the children are able to learn many new words thus expanding their vocabulary, and learn sentence structures and develop problem solving skills. It has been observed that the children with very short attention span concentrate for a longer time when engrossed in a story. Through contextual stories, we can acquaint children with their culture, social norms and create awareness about their surroundings.

Teachers while narrating the stories orally, the teachers should know the story well and the stories should be narrated with voice modulation and expressions. A very well told story will help the children visualize and participate in the event that are unfolding through the story.

The books should be always used by the teachers while telling the story. The reason is that the child needs to know how to read and enjoy books touching them, turning pages, looking at pictures, figure reading – this would encourage the child at all times.

The pictures in the books support content and retain the interest of children. Here when the children see that the teacher is reading stories from the books then they would understand the importance of the print media and the books and the need and the value of reading as a skill.

Use of puppetry this can be ready made or even made by the teacher with the help of the children this can be used to narrate stories. This may be stick puppets, glove puppets, finger puppets, box puppets and so on, this would motivate the child and help them develop creativity among the children.

Flash cards that have some story scenes either drawn or printed on them can be used to tell stories. They may be larger than a book and also easy to hold. Flash cards can also serve as a sequence of cards that can be given to the children to organize and display it in a proper order.

Here the selection of a story makes a lot of difference. Really speaking the selection of the story is very critical, the story should be age appropriate, familiar in language and it should be interesting for the children. The stories should be used to reinforce important learning objectives such as developing sensitivity to others and good work habits and inculcate core values and the important relationships and so on.

Finally, after telling the story the teacher should be able to find out whether the children have understood the content of the story, for which the teacher should be able to ask few questions of what, whom, why, where, how, and what if. As the children are growing older the teacher can change the question as this discuss why a character behave in a certain way, what was the consequences and so on.

3. Toy –Based Learning

This is one of the most important activity under the play way pedagogy. It is very well understood that the young children mostly learn from first hand experiences and working with actual objects. Most of the children are seen to try out things by trial and error method and by doing so they explore things and then learn from them. For this type of learning we will have to cultivate and develop our class room environment in such a way so that the children should develop the spirit of exploration through playing with toys and try to manipulate things and develop new ideas. Now there are several toys available to the child in their vicinity, now how the child could use them under the guidance of their teacher and make use of it as a resourceful object for the teaching and learning purpose.

Whenever, a child holds a toy then the child tries to manipulate it, that is the child is trying to practice her motor skills and trying to strengthening her hand –eye coordination. The toys that require children to push, pull, grab, pinch, turn, or otherwise use their hands and body to make it do something are instrumental for the child's growth. During the play with their toys the children will try to learn new ideas constantly by thinking and rethinking on it. Thus the child learns to overcome the difficulties which the child comes in her earlier attempts. Thus the child slowly learns from by making small mistakes earlier and then they try to correct them.

4. Songs and Rhymes

Children love singing songs and rhymes and dancing to music. Songs and the rhymes are the wonderful means of learning language. It has been seen in most of the schools we see that the children are taught to recite rhymes in English and Hindi and it is through that the children are able to learn the required language that is English and Hindi. We have to select the song or rhymes in such a way so that they could support the concept that the children need to learn. The songs can be used to learn about the animals, their movements, being careful, getting hurt, the duties of a doctor, and counting. Singing and acting on these songs would make the children happy and have fun.

It has been understood that the body movements and gestures enacted by the children would help the children in understanding the concepts of the lessons. It is also understood that most of the children are able to understand different concepts through songs and it helps in the improvement of their vocabulary. The student's physical movements accompanying the songs would enhance the gross and fine motor muscle movements and gestures help children in understanding concepts. It has been understood that the song also promotes interactions among the children and this also leads to peer co-operations.

5. Music and Movement

As per the scientific studies carried out in Germany, it has been proved beyond doubt that the Music is one of the strong stimulation for the brain development and also it helps in the formation of synaptic connections. It has also been proved that the listening of Indian classical music has a soothing effect on the brain and helps in proper development of the brain. So, the following rhythm and playing simple musical instruments, and singing should be encouraged. This would help the children to have body movements which can be accompanied by clapping or rhythm played on any musical instrument.

Children right from the fetal stage keep listening to various types of sounds around them in various forms. In the child when in the fetal stage, they often listen to the conversation of their parents. It is because of this reason the newly born child doesn't react to the voices of the parents as to them it is a familiar voice. But when the newly born child listen to a new strange voice then they will look towards the origin of the voice strangely.

It is a regular sight in the musical class of the small children where the teacher sings a song then the children repeat the same. In most of the preprimary classes it has been seen that the children are made to sing the song with action, gestures and some body movements. The children are also seen singing the song in groups or in pairs or individually.

Music and movements activities can be done in different ways. For instance, the children may be asked to listen to the music played on instrument. The children could also be encouraged to dance freely to the rhythm of the music.

The children should also be encouraged to make or design their own musical instrument. Small children are capable to do that; I have seen the children in class fourth was able to play music by preparing Jal Tharang by filling different layers of water in glass bowls and then playing the same with two sticks which generates very good music. What is required is the motivation and the guidance of the music teacher.

Children are naturally attracted to the sound of musical instruments and enjoy playing drums, bells, etc. the children should be encouraged to play musical instruments right from the young age. This would encourage the children to develop innovative skills and this interest to music would help the children to keep themselves away from stress and help in the brain development.

6. Arts and Craft

It is our common observation that the children do enjoy playing with color's and creating something what makes them interesting. Here the arts and craft would provide another medium for the children to express their own ideas, emotions and feelings. These may be in the form of drawing, painting, pasting, clay modelling, Rangoli etc.

i. **Drawing:** Here the children are seen to make use of paper and crayons, sketch pens, coloured or black pencils or charcoal. It has been observed that the children make use of the black board, slate, floor, and some children are seen drawing and painting on the walls. Drawing is a very important activity in which the children are able to express their own ideas which are expressed by them. This activity also help the children to develop a very fine motor coordination.

ii. **Painting:** Painting is an activity through which the children are exploring the use of wet colour on paper, floor or fabric. Here the children make use of brushes which are available in the market. Through these painting we are able to understand the views of the child and his thought and his views of the world. It has been seen that most of the children spend hours together in this activity.

iii. **Pasting:** The pasting mainly involves the use of glue and thing that can be used for sticking on paper and fabric. The children usually draw sketch on the paper or fabric and paste matchsticks or coloured paper or it can be a free pasting activity. A collage using different materials can also be created.

iv. **Clay Modelling:** Here the children are seen to make use of the wet clay or potters clay for clay moulding. The dough is made by the teacher and provided to the children the children are hereby encouraged to explore this medium and create different shapes and objects. As an extension of the activity, the clay objects created by the children can be dried and painted on a later day. I have seen in some of the schools the students are able to prepare idols of Ganapati or Lord Ganesh and a good model of Dr. B. R. Ambedkar.

V. **Rangoli:** Rangoli is one of the activity which has been seen to be carried out by the children, it has been seen that the boys and the girls do take active part in this activity. The children are able to draw an outline and then fill in colours on the lay out. The children are seen to come out with various their own ideas and theme for the Rangoli created by them.

7. Dramatics

Dramatics is an important activity which can be carried out in the class room as well as at the school level. Dramatics thus performed should be able to convey a proper message or it should be hilarious for the children. The drama or the piece of the drama which has been selected should be according to the mental state or level of the child and it should also carry a message or must be having a learning significance also. The story of the play should be well scripted as per their age and mental state. The story of the play should be given to one child and the child is free to express themselves accordingly. Here the teacher can work as a guide and show some guideline and cannot interfere in any way of expression, in pronunciation or in anything else connected with the use of the mother tongue. The children should be encouraged to take part in these type of activities. Apart from these they should also be encouraged to take part in mock trials, or mock interview, and so on.

8. Magazines

It is my observation in some of the well set schools the students are made to work on class magazine and the school magazines. Where the students are seen contributing write-ups on various topics of their own interest. The magazines thus developed are seen to be displayed for the parents and other visitors in the school at prominent place. The basic idea is to demonstrate the students achievement and their contribution to show their creativity to the visitors and the parent. The children are made to write articles on various topics of their interest so that it can be displayed in the magazine this may be a class magazine or the school magazine. This activity would boost the children's interest towards writing, their contribution may be in English, Hindi or in their own mother tongue every child in the class is expected to make their contribution, but only care that needs to be taken is that the children select the topic of their contribution in a proper manner. If at all there is any financial problem, then it can be written by the children who has a good hand writing and discussed in the class so that the participants would be encouraged. The development of the magazine whether it is a class magazine of the school magazine it is a good creative device in using the play way method. Therefore; it is essential that each school should have both the class and the school magazine published, this is to be done only to develop the creative talents of the children.

9. Indoor Games

Games are essential for the general development of the child. the nature of games may differ according to the level of intelligence of the child. here, it is important to highlight the various devices used in for different classes, playing in teaching primary classes. Games are most important for developing intelligence among the children. During the childhood period, the children are not in a position to receive direct instructions. However, they are interested in learning through different types of games and activities. Some such games and activities are suggested below:

a) Pictures

Here the children are shown a picture with a large number of objects in it, and they are required to write down all the names of the objects in the picture accordingly or they may be asked to detect any one particular object among all the objects present in the picture. This is the very principle that is applied to the kindergarten school these days.

b) Matching Board

The matching boards are prepared with letters or word in horizontal lines and below each letter or the word, a space is left empty. The children have a sets of letters or words. They are required to select their sets corresponding to the first one on the board, and put in the space on the board under the first letter or word.

c) Flashing Card

This is a card which is shown by a child to a group of children or the child of another group for two seconds and then he is asked what is written on it. If the child says the word correctly, then the child who asked the question comes to the other group and vice versa. The group which has more member's wins in the competition.

d) Passing an Order

In this game the class is made to be seated in a large circle. The teacher will whisper a sentence or an order to the first child. then the first child will whisper exactly what he has heard to the next child and so on right round the circle. Then at the end, the child in the last will say what he has heard.

e) Word Building

This is a game which is used to build a word when a child says one word using the letter given by another child.

f) Spelling Games

This is a game in which the child is asked to spell the word as quickly as possible when it is said to him or her.

g) Making Sentences

This is a game in which the children are directed to frame the sentence using the words provided by the teacher. This is a very good language game. In this statement making game, it is for the teacher to put up on the black board a number of words. The children are then asked to make as many sentence as possible using only those words but using them as often as they like.

h) Finding the Stranger

In this game a list of words is given in which one word is not linked to the other words. It will be detected by the child as stranger in the line.

i) Description Game

In this game the teacher describes some object without mentioning the name. the class has to guess what the object is. Play way in teaching middle classes.

1. The Story Game

In this game the teacher can present the facts before the children in the form of a story. The children are welcome to appreciate the story and also say the similar events.

2. Description Game

In this game the whole class is divided into two groups. Two different things decided by these two groups but one member of each group must remain outside. So they will be stranger to the decision of the group. The game starts with one child would speak a sentence on the decision so that the stranger can know about the decision taken. If he fails another students speaks another statement. If one child fails, to understand the decision, then he will be out from the game. In this way, this game continues.

3. Question Game

Here in this game the class is divided into two groups. Questions are asked between the two groups and marks are allotted to the groups that gives the correct answer. Here the child is given two related terms, i.e., one word is related to the other. But in case of blank, giving only one word, the child has to fill up the blank taking clue from the given pair. Lastly, it is more accepted as it stresses on the use of the three H's – Hand, Heart and Head. It makes the teaching –learning processes more active one which is the basic idea of educational setting.

4. Outdoor Games

The outdoor games are very important for the children to develop the gross motor skills. The outdoor games could be anything like walking, running, jumping, chasing, kicking, throwing balls, playing in water or sand or mud, crawling through tunnels etc. these would help the children to develop their motor skills. The teacher should be able to use the bricks and make the children to balance themselves and walk. The teachers should be able to provide play materials like the big ball, rings, hoola hoop and rope jumping.

The younger children can play group games with no rules or with simple rules. During the games it important that the teacher keeps an eye for the safety of the children and should ensure that no children are injured.

The Merits of the Play Way Method of Teaching

1. Playing is a natural process for children. So, a child activity involves in it, and the child gets pleasure and satisfaction.

2. Similarly, at the same time learning takes place naturally through play way method.

3. Opportunity is given to a child for full participation in this method.

4. It not only develops the knowledge skill of children, but also brings satisfaction in their cognitive level.

5. It also paves way for self-discipline.

6. It gives more opportunities for children's learning with perception and mind.

The Demerits of the Play Way Method of Teaching

1. This method is more suitable for the pre-primary and primary level children only.

2. The contents and the concepts of all subjects cannot be introduced in this method.

3. Few children may give more importance to playing games than learning through play way method.

4. At present, realizing the importance of the play way method and its use for different levels of teaching, it is introduced from the preschool stage onwards. Good planning and efforts of the teacher makes the application of this method a successful one.

CHAPTER 5

Pedagogy of Teaching Children at the Foundational Stage

The word pedagogy in a simpler term it can be described as the act of teaching. The pedagogy adopted by the teachers mainly shapes their actions, judgements, and the teaching strategies by taking into consideration of the theories of learning, understanding of the students and their needs and the backgrounds and interests of individual students. Pedagogy in other word is for education – the profession and science of teaching.

A safe, secure, comfortable and a happy class room environment could always help children to learn better and also help them to achieve much more at the foundational stage. An utmost care and responsiveness with ample opportunities to experience, experiment and exploration are the hallmarks of pedagogy at their stage. The principles of pedagogy under lay all decisions related to teaching strategies in the class room appropriate for the foundational stage.

One of the most important factor for the class room planning and instruction is a safe and stimulating environment is one of the fundamental to development and learning at this foundational stage. Here we have to plan up activities which are joyful and encourage the use of all the child's senses. The class room teaching provides variety of challenges. The physical and the emotional safety is paramount while making any pedagogical choices. The class room should be clean, cheerful, well ventilated, and well –lit learning space.

The play is to be the central to learning and development at this stage. This play can be free, guided or structured, various activities such as conversations, stories, music, various types of movements, arts, craft, toys, and games are a part of play and these methods are to engage children in play, where as many other methods can be innovated. The outdoor play should also be encouraged. Nurturing relationship between the teacher and the child is necessary and being with them is important as they are the basis of teaching and learning. The class room activities have to be encouraged, the gross and fine motor skills, physical movements do help the child to have a socio emotional and cognitive development, in fact the physical development of the child is very important at this stage.

We should be aware of the fact that every child learns at their own pace and learning needs are to be addressed individually. Opportunities needs to be provided for all children alike and they should be allowed to participate in the class room in ways that suit each child the best. It has to be noted that the children learn well and seem to be comfortable and learn the best in their home language. The transition from home language to school language is gentle and always scaffolder by the home language. The children should be allowed to express themselves as much as possible and never judge or reprimanded for the language that they speak. Make sure that the learning experiences in the class room are deeply connected to the children's lives and their context. They extensively use the local stories, rhyme, songs, games, crafts, material are regularly used. the learning lessons and experiences and planned and designed to build on children's previous understanding, here the planning moves from the simple to complex ideas and they build concepts based on this principle by using the home language. The class room activities should be so planned that it would address all the domains of development.

Planning a Requisite for Teaching

As we are all aware of the fact that teaching is an act that needs to be carried out with a proper intention of bringing about learning among children. This act has to be well planned and planning should be the main center to good teaching. Here the word planning includes construction and organization of class room tasks as per competencies and outcomes to be achieved, pedagogy needs to be followed, resources to be used and assessment to be carried out. Planning should also include support activities for children, home assignments and display in the class relevant to what is being taught.

Planning is an exercise that needs to be done on a yearly basis when it has to be carried out, or for a term or for a week, for the day, and it can be done for one lesson also. The teacher must plan for the week, the day and even for one lesson.

A good planning does require a proper understanding of the curricular goals, competencies and learning outcomes to be achieved along with prior learning of the children for whom the plan is being made, and available teaching, learning material and content to be used.

The major components of the teaching plans are as follows:

1. It is essential that the teacher should have a better knowledge about the competencies, learning out comes, and the intended lessons and its objectives.

2. The teaching should be teacher directed, teacher guided and child let activities to achieve objectives.

3. There should be a specific duration and there should be a sequence of activities.

4. There should be a specific content and suitable material to be used in the activities.

5. There should be a proper class room arrangement. i.e., seating arrangement, displays, and arrangement of materials.

6. The teacher should be able to derive specific strategies for the children who needs extra help.

7. The teacher should also have a proper method of assessment.

Important Stages for Planning

1. Planning for a Differentiated Instruction

A teacher will have to plan her class in such a way that she is able to engage the class children with varying interest and capabilities meaningfully and encourage them for a better learning. One way is by thinking about this in a differentiated way of instruction. This can be done by tailoring the teaching processes according to the individual needs of the children. Here the content method of learning material and assessment may be different for different children. It is a different task to do it for individual children especially in a large class, under such condition the teacher will have to identify children in to small groups who have similar needs and address them differently as a group. Before such planning, it is important for the teacher to observe the children carefully and gather much information as possible about them and then plan the activities that needs to be taken.

2. Scaffolding and Gradual Release of Responsibility

Children are capable of learning new knowledge easily when they are provided systematic support from experienced children or adults. Learning new knowledge should be a challenge, but the challenge should be within the reach of the children. Something that relates to their existing knowledge and this can be done with the support of an experienced person.

To learn the children needs systematic scaffolding. Scaffolding refers to providing support, structure and guidance during instruction. This scaffolding can be provided through a "gradual release of responsibility" (GRR), where first, teachers model or explain ideas or skills, after which children and teachers work together on the same ideas and skills where the teachers provides guided support, and finally the children practices individually and independently.

Studies has shown that this method works well for literacy and numeracy learning but it is important to remember that every skill of literacy or numeracy cannot be learnt in this way. The teachers may use their judgement on what could work best in their class room and built it into their teaching plan.

3. **Home Work**

Home work is an event that should not happen at this foundational stage. In fact for the children at this foundational stage the home work should be filled with fun and it should be able to provide a different kind of interesting challenge for the teacher. The home work should be planned in such a way that the school should get connected with the child's home. This type of activities can be planned by the teachers only after children are well settled in the school and have got into a comfortable routine. When doing this task the teachers should ensure that the children can do these tasks on their own. It should be ensured that the parents or others should not do anything on their behalf.

Creating a Positive Relationship Between Teacher And Children

It is my observation that when we walk into a class room were newly admitted children are there. We will have a strange feeling. It is observed that some children are not willing to sit in the class and they want to go back home with their parents. Some children are seen screaming in the class and shouting calling mummy or papa and so on. At the same time there are some students who would sit quietly in the class and see the fun going on in the class. They are seen observing and is interested in everything going around them. Some of them constantly asking questions to the teachers, where as some children keep observing other children, in a matter of minutes those children who were silent, they too loose interest and after some time they also starts crying. At the same time there are students who keep on moving around, jumping on desks and benches and they keep enjoying themselves. Some of them cry and clamour to go home, whereas some needs to be comforted and cajoled and are willing to be convinced to stay back. They are very curious and considerate, delightful, determined, affectionate and adventurous, funny and fearless.

For many of the children this would be their first experience of spending hours away from their homes. Children requires tenderness, nurturing and love. Working with them, being with them, caring for them, means enjoying all the very different personalities that they are.

Here the teachers need to be warm and genuine, patient and calm, understanding and empathetic – we need to give our children unhurried time and attention. The children should feel that they belong, they can trust, they must feel free to act and explore and therefore learn better.

As a teacher our job is to ensure that the children settle and enjoy their time at school. A safe and a positive relationship between the teacher and the children is built. This relationship between teacher and the child is enriching both the emotional and cognitive development. Here are some important means to build a positive relationship, and they are as under: -

a) The first most important factor, is that the teacher and the child should be able to know each other i.e. the teacher should be able to know each and every child individually about their home, their family and members in the family, to know their interests, things what they do outside the school, their pets, their favorite people. This helps the teacher to understand each child and then this will help them to plan learning experiences for each of them.

b) Listening to children – it is an important fact that the teacher is able to listen to their stories, their narrations of what happens at home, their opinions and views on everything that interests them this conveys care and respects, builds trusts, help children think and communicates, and gain confidence.

c) Keep observing the children consciously – when the children are observed continuously and it is important that the teacher keep on interacting with the children, this may help us to discover how much the child thinks, reasons and responds to different situations, which is really critical to planning for the teaching and learning.

d) Encouraging the children's intuitional response – Here the words, actions, solving a small problem, analyzing what happened – all this helps to a meaningfully build on children's naturally creative and resourcefulness.

e) Recognizing and responding to the emotions and moods of children – it is through conversation, music, storytelling, arts, playing together are some of the activities that would help the children to settle down better, learn better, learn slowly regulate their own emotions, and begin to understand and respond to the emotions of others.

f) Visiting their homes regularly – this is an important activity so as to understand children and their home environment and build trust and this creates a positive bond.

How Can the Teachers Support Children to Learn Better?

The aim of the early learning class room is to enhance the children learning and development through activities and play. Here the teachers play a crucial role in supporting the children in many ways. Some of the means are described here below.

1. Listening

It becomes the duty of every teacher to listen to and attend to the young child's conversations, enquiries, questions and theories about the world. For instance, if the child says, that a spider has many eyes, here the teacher may need to speak and emphasizes the same; "yes, you are right", a spider has many eyes'. how did you know that? This tells the child that the teacher has heard, acknowledged, and is helping extend the topic. The teacher may further guide them to a book on insects, share a fact or show a video expanding their curiosity and learning.

2. Modelling

One of the ways through which the children learn is through observation and imitation. Here the teachers need to consciously model different behaviour for children to pick up new concepts and skills. For example, the teacher while teaching one to one correspondence for pre numeracy, then teacher can take five coins and five stones, and show exactly how every coin corresponds to a stone and tell the children the corresponding number. The teacher can say one stone one coin, two stone – two coin and so on, while counting and pointing. The children will see and repeat this. Similar modelling would occur in all routine behaviour, songs, actions, clay word pronunciations and so on. The teachers must be alert to what they are saying and doing in the presence of the children.

3. Exploring

It is our observation that the children are often curious, constantly engaged to trial and error and exploring new things. When the children play with blocks, cardboard or even in sand, they are trying to solve simple problems. How much water to be added to the sand to make it a good sand mould. How to stick cardboard such that it can form a curve or not get unstuck. How to place blocks or dominoes such that the tower or domino sequences does not break. The teacher provides scaffolds to the child in the form of questions. Or physical support or an idea to solve the puzzle such scaffolding help children imagine and think through solutions on their own.

4. Questioning

Children think while verbalizing their ideas at that time a question from the teacher will help them to think through a particular subject in depth in a particular angle while responding. This also support language development. For example, asking why did you put the big block at the base? Will help the children verbalize the reason behind a choice they have made. It is important for the teacher to be attentive to what children are doing in their play activities and ask relevant questions.

5. Provoking

Challenging children ways of knowing, thinking and doing deepens their understanding of the world around. Children lend to pick up stereotypical notions based on what they see and hear around them. The teacher needs to be proactive to questions, to provoke and provide alternate perspectives e.g., picking a story that talks about the capabilities of a child with disability or women as bus drivers or pilots.

6. Researching

Teachers needs to provide children with tools and skills to learn how to understand their inquiry into a topic –where to look. Whom to ask, what to use for solving questions and arriving at some understanding. Teachers themselves need to practice researching in order to understanding children better, respond to their queries, and develop and conduct new activates to enhance children's learning.

7. Making Children Independence

Planning well helps teachers take active steps with children to make them independent – first closely work with them gradually release support to make them confident in a new skill or a new understanding.

CHAPTER 6

Inquiry Based Science Education

In the previous chapters we have come across this word or phrase Inquiry based education. Now in this chapter let us look into the details of this methodology which is mainly used in the teaching of science in most of the school around the globe, but the same is very sparingly used in our country. However, this is an important methodology which needs to be to be used to bring up our children properly in science education. By the implementation if this method we can motivate our children towards learning science. Even though we have a larger youth population in our country but the number of children taking science as their field of education is very low as compared to the children in developed countries. It is now important that we are able to motivate more and more children towards he learning of science in our country.

Now, let us imagine a baby who is able to crawl on the ground is put in an isolated room with some tools or attractively coloured toys to play with and he is not attended too by anybody. If we are able to observe and study the child's activity carefully then we can see that the child will approach the toys or the objects, move around and then slowly touch the object, and then try to pull it or drag it, beat it, and once he is sure that the object is safe to handle and play then the child would start playing with it until the child is disturbed by anybody or till the child is hungry. Have you ever visualized this phenomenon? Have you ever questioned the reason why the child is acting in this way? Every child or the toddler will always make sure that the new object that is provided to him is safe and secure to touch and handle it or play with it. In an experiment performed by me, the infant was provided an object which gave very mild shock. When the child touched the same object the child received a mild shock and the child cried out loudly. Thereafter, whenever the child sees the same object or whenever the child was provided with the same object the child did not touch the object but the child started crying loudly. This is due to fear or scare of the object. This shows that the infants too have the ability to understand and learn things, and they do so by the touch and by feeling it. Thus experiencing things is an act of learning by doing things. Thus the art of learning science by the child when the children are not attended too can be called as the inquiry based science education.

I have put in many years of science teaching in a very reputed school in India. During these years of my teaching experience, I have seen that the children do have the ability of preparing the science topics of their own, when any portion of the topic is left out by the teacher with some intention; this may be due to punishment or with the instruction to the children to prepare for a seminar etc. they are able to prepare the topic well and their achievement in that topic would be much more better than those topics which have been taught and covered by the teacher in a regular class room teaching. In fact, what I could understand is that the children are able to learn and do things better when they are not attended too or guided by the teacher or anybody. They are capable to find out the required knowledge and the information from various available sources such as the internet, library, from the fields, or by performing their own experiments and then submit their report or write ups in a proper and in a systematic way by consulting their teacher, or with the help of their senior colleagues, friends, parents etc. such an act by the child would have various impact on the child. The child will be able to understand the concept in a proper way, the child would also be able to learn the sequences and the order how things are needed to be put up or presented in a proper manner. Not only that the child will be able to master the subject or the topic in a better way, when the child is able to collect the required information and knowledge by himself for his own study. This type of work is called as the learning by inquiry method which is carried out by the child, does have the following significance –

1. The children shall be able to perform their own experiments without any guidance of the teacher or any adults. By doing so the children will be able to master the methodology very well in a systematic and in a stepwise manner. This will also help the children to

develop their own skills in a better way than what they acquire when they are guided by a teacher.

2. The children would be able to master the required techniques of collecting the data or references from various available sources themselves, such as by visiting the library, browsing the internet, referring the various journals, etc. by doing so, they would also be able to master the method of cataloging this information in a systematic way for future use, and they also learn the method of making notes and briefs before they are able to perform the experiments.

3. The children would be able to properly master and learn the techniques, the theory, the basic principle of the experimentation and the stepwise procedures, well in advance before they are able to perform the experiments.

4. The children would be able to learn and develop the art of cooperative learning and working and they would be able to carry out discussions on the experiments carried out by them and then finally come to a proper conclusion about the results obtained by them after performing the experiments.

5. The children shall learn to be disciplined when working in the laboratory. The children would always be disciplined when they realize that their teacher or their supervisor is not in the laboratory.

6. This methodology of teaching would provoke the child to think and come out with new innovative and creative ideas, this may help the child to come out with new ideas and this would even lead to new discoveries or new findings.

What is the science of inquiry? Well this can be defined as a scientific methodology and that is *"active, persistent, and careful in consideration of any belief or supposed form of knowledge in the light of the grounds that support it and the further conclusions to which it tends."* Here the word grounding of "any belief" mainly occurs through an inquiry processes such as: reasoning, evidences, inferences and generalization. However, today the modern science educations have proposed various lists of an inquiry process and these mainly includes - observations, measuring, predicting, inferring, using numbers, using space-time relationships, defining operationally, formulating hypotheses, interpreting data, controlling variables, experimenting and communicating.

In a country like India, were we are using the traditional method of teaching; that is, the chalk and talk method is more common. Under these conditions the introduction of the inquiry method of science teaching would be very difficult. The reason here is for using this methodology of teaching the teacher should be well equipped and prepared with the latest developments and well informed and up to date in his or her subject and should be constantly reading and updating their knowledge. It's than only, the teacher will be able to properly guide the children in a proper way in the inquiry based learning. While working or learning through this inquiry based method the children may encounter several problems, which needs a solution or guidance from the teacher, hence, it's essential that the teacher is up to date with his or her own subject matter and capable to guide the child.

It has been seen that during the processes of inquiry based learning most of the children always face and encounter problems that would be perplexing and even may cause great discomfort; and such discomforting problems would be the real essence of activities caused by scientific inquiry. Studies on educational research carried out in the United States and elsewhere in the developing countries have shown that the children do well by learning science through the inquiry method. It has also been observed that the children become very effective and their performance is also found to be better and enhanced. The children are also seen to develop better skills and attitudes, and they are found to score better in their achievement tests, a positive attitude is seen developing in them, the children are seen participating in the scientific inquiry and these children always leads to a positive analytical and critical thinking and show and high order of skill development.

Though it has been proved that the inquiry method of teaching is one of the best methodologies in the teaching of science but the same cannot be implemented in the school level in our country. The teachers too are not ready to implement this methodology in the teaching and learning processes of sciences in our schools due to the following reasons:

- Most of the science teachers in our country is not in position to implement the inquiry method of teaching because they are not exposed to this methodology of teaching. They to lack the skills and the strategies for the implementation of the inquiry method of teaching in our class room even at the secondary level.

- Most of our teachers feel that the inquiry based method of teaching is difficult to manage, as the laboratories in the schools do not have sufficient equipment's and the materials to implement the inquiry based method of teaching in our Indian schools.

- It is a general belief that the Science education by the inquiry based method of teaching does not work well for all the children in India. It is believed that this would work well for the bright and gifted children. It is also believed that this method may create lot of problems for those children who are considered to be below average children.

- The method of science education by enquiry based education is not possible in those schools run in rural areas as these rural schools don't even have a proper Science laboratory conditions were these children are not able to carry out experimentations in their schools.

What is Inquiry?

Apart from the above given definition, the term inquiry can also be defined as an active pursuit of meaningful involvement in a thoughtful process that can change experiences into bits of knowledge. Inquiry method is mainly modeled on the scientific method of discovery. It can be viewed that the science as a constructed set of theories and ideas that is based on the physical world rather than on the collection of irrefutable and disconnected facts. It can also focus on asking questions, considering alternative explanations, and weighing it based on the evidence.

Let us take an example, when you are walking, you come across a strange type of an object, by seeing that you remain astonished and puzzled. This may raise several questions in your mind, such as; what is it? How it has come into being? What is it made up of? What are its uses? And so on. With a curiosity to know the answer, what it is? You may approach the object and carefully watch it, and to know whether the object can be moving, i.e., whether the object is living or non-living? Once you have made it sure that it is not harmful then you touch it and then subject the object for various test. Then you will have to compare this object with another object and make a comparison or make a comparative study. Later you may have to make enquiries with your friends, and the people around you with an aim to understand the object and to know how it has originated and how it has reached this spot and then formulate some theories that could make some type of sense. All these activities involve careful observation, theorizing, experimenting, and testing of theories etc. and all these are a part and parcel of the inquiry methodology. Thus the main purpose of this activity is to gather enough information about something and to put together all the theories collected together in a proper order so, that it will make new experiences which would be less strange and more meaningful.

Characteristics of Inquiry

Inquiry is a term that is used in science teaching and that refers to a way of questioning, seeking knowledge or information, or finding out about some phenomena. Many science teachers throughout the globe have advocated that science teaching should emphasize through inquiry based method. It is needed for an effective science teaching and it is the same as what was used during the effective scientific investigation. Thus the methods that is used by scientists in their research should be the same as an integral part of the methods which needs to be used in the science teaching classrooms in our schools. In fact we might think of the method of scientific investigation as the process of inquiry in the class room teaching. Now to know the process of inquiry based teaching there are five important characteristics that has been identified and they are as follows:

- *Observation*: Science always begins with the observation of matter or any phenomena. It is the starting place for an inquiry. However, asking the right questions would guide the observer to a crucial aspect of the process of observation.

- *Measurement:* Quantitative description of the objects and phenomena is an essential accepted for the practice of science, and it becomes desirable because of the value in science on precision and accurate description.

- *Experimentation:* Experiments are designed mainly to test the questions and the ideas, and as such they are the cornerstone of science. Experiments involve questions, observations and measurements.

- *Communication:* The Communication of the results to the scientific community and to the public is an obligation for the scientist, and this is also an essential part of the inquiry process. The values of independent thinking and truthfulness in reporting the results of all the observations and measurements are essential and in this regard. As pointed out earlier in the section on the nature of science, the "republic of science" is dependent on the communication to all its members. Generally, it is done by publishing an articles in journals, and the same is discussed in the professional meetings and seminars.

- *Mental Processes:* Several thinking processes that are the integral part of the scientific inquiry: the inductive reasoning, formulating hypotheses and theories, deductive reasoning, as well as analogy, extrapolation, synthesis and finally evaluation. The mental processes of scientific inquiry may also include other processes such as the use of imagination and intuition.

Inquiry Based Education for Class Room Teaching

The inquiry based teaching should be a method in which need to be adapted for grade 9th to grade 12th in our schools. So that the children are able to develop the required scientific abilities which would be characterized within them the sense of scientific inquiry, and they could participate effectively in the required scientific investigations and they are able to use their cognitive and manipulative skills associated with formulation of scientific explanations.

The children at this stage should be able to understand that the experiments are guided by concepts and they are performed to test the ideas. It has been observed that some children still have the difficulties in understanding the variables and the role of controlled experiments. They do have trouble in dealing with data that seem anomalous and in proposing explanations based on evidence and logic.

The greatest success of this inquiry method of teaching lies on how the child masters the concept that guides the inquiry, and the child's acquisition of knowledge, which is based on to support the child's investigation so as to develop a suitable scientific explanation for the concept of the world the child brings to school. This will shape the way as the children get involved in the science investigation. This would develop a deeper insight for the child in understanding science in a true sense. The child should be exposed to full inquiry, instructional strategy which should involve small group discussions, labeled drawings, writings and concept mappings, etc. which will have to be guided by the teacher so that the children, work can be presented with all the information in a proper presentable form. The child's explanation which comes from the presentation prepared by the child becomes the baseline for the instruction and the teacher should help the children to align it with the scientific knowledge.

The children should also learn how to analyses the available evidences and the data which is available to the child. The evidences which they would analyses, may be from their own investigation or from the data obtained from the investigations of other children or from the data which is available in the databases. The strategies of data manipulation and analyses needs to be modeled by the teacher and the same will have to be practiced by the children. Determining the range of the data, the mean and mode values of the data, plotting of the data, developing the mathematical functions from the data, and looking for anomalous data are all examples of the analyses that are performed by the children. It is essential that the science teacher keep on raising the questions, such as "how confident are you with the data?" "Do you feel that these data are accurate?" "What explanation do you expect from these data?"

Public presentation of the experiment performed by the child is very essential to develop in the child a moral boost and confidence in them. This will help the children know the art of presentation of the paper or the investigation performed by the child boldly before the audience. This can be done at the school level also in the form of a peer review. Talking with the peer about the science experiments performed by the child would help the children to develop proper meaning and understanding. Their conversation would clarify that the concepts and processes of science, thus helping the children to make sense of the contents of science. During the peer review of the work done by the children, the science teacher should engage the children in conversations that focus on questions, such as "how do we know?" "Is the evidences provided by you enough to draw this conclusion?" "Do we need more evidences?" "is there any other method that can be used in this investigation?" These questions would make the child to think further and to analyses the data, develop a richer knowledge data base? The child shall be able to reason them by using the science concepts, make relationships between evidence and explanations, and recognize alternative explanations.

The Abilities Required by the Child for Doing Scientific Inquiry

1. To identify questions and concepts that guide scientific investigations:

The children should be able to formulate a testable hypothesis of their own and demonstrate a logical connection between the scientific concepts guiding a hypothesis and the design of an experiment. They should be able to demonstrate appropriate procedures, a knowledge base and conceptual understanding of the scientific investigations.

2. The child should be capable of designing and conduct of scientific investigations:

   The child should be capable of designing and conducting of the scientific investigations which requires introduction of the major concepts into the areas being investigated, arranging proper equipment, safety precautions, seeking assistance with methodological problems, recommendations for use of technologies, clarification of ideas that guide the inquiry and scientific knowledge obtained from sources other than the actual investigation. The investigation may require the children for the clarification of the question, method, controls, and variables, the children organization and display of data, the children revision of methods and explanations and a public presentation of the results thus obtained with a critical response from peers. Regardless of all the scientific investigations performed, children must be able to use evidence, apply logic, and construct an argument for their proposed explanation.

3. Use of modern technology and Mathematical imputation to improve investigations and communications:

Today we have a variety of modern technologies that are available, such as the hand tools, measuring instruments, calculators, these things today form an integral component of a scientific investigations. The use of computers for the collection, analyses and display of the data is a part of this standards. Mathematics plays an important role in all aspects of an inquiry. For example, measurement is used for posing questions, formulas are used for developing explanations and the chart and graphs are used for the communication of the results.

4. Formulation and revise scientific explanations and models using logic and evidences:

   The child's inquiry should always culminate in formulating an explanation or model. The models should be physical, conceptual, and mathematical. In the process of answering the questions, the children should engage in discussions and arguments based on the result in the revision of their explanations. These discussions should be based on scientific knowledge, the use of logic, and evidences from their scientific investigation.

5. Recognise and analyse alternative explanations and models:

   This aspect of the standard emphasizes the critical abilities of analyzing an argument by reviewing current scientific understanding, weighing the evidence, and examining the logic so as to decide which explanations and models are the best. In other words, although there may be several plausible explanations they do not at all have equal weight. Children should be able to use scientific criteria to find the preferred explanations.

6. Communicate and defend a scientific argument:

Children in school science programs should emphasis the critical abilities that are associated with accurate and effective communication. These include writing and following procedures, expressing concepts, reviewing information, summarizing data, using language appropriately, developing diagrams and charts, explaining statistical analysis, speaking clearly and logically, constructing a reasoned argument, and responding appropriately to a critical comment.

Developing the Child's Understanding About Scientific Inquiry

This is one of the most difficult aspects for a teacher in the school. The teacher will have to make things very clear to the children by way of giving explanations, the need of scientific inquiry based method and this should cover up the entire major phenomenon that needs to be done during the processes of scientific inquiry based method. The teacher should also brief the children that the -

> ➤ Scientists usually inquire about, how physical, living or designed systems function. The conceptual principles and knowledge guide the scientific inquiry processes.

Historical and the current scientific knowledge would only influence in the design and interpretations of the investigations and the evaluation of proposed explanations made by other scientists.

➢ A scientist conducts investigations for a wide variety of reasons. For example, they may wish to discover new aspects of the natural phenomenon occurring around the world, want to explain the recently observed phenomenon, or test the conclusions of the prior investigations that are carried out by other scientists or to challenge the predications or the findings of the current theories.

➢ The scientists rely on the technologies to enhance the gathering and manipulations of data. The scientist applies new techniques and tools that provide new evidences to guide the inquiry and this new method to gather data, thus, by contributing to the advancement of science. The accuracy and precision of the data, and therefore the quality of the exploration, depends on the type of technology used.

➢ Mathematics is essential in scientific inquiry. Mathematical tools and models guide and improve the posing of questions, gathering data, constructing explanations and communication of the results.

➢ The scientific explanation must adhere to the following criteria such as:

✓ Proposed explanation must be logically consistent;

✓ It must abide with the rules of evidence;

✓ it must be open to questions and possible modification;

✓ And, it must be based on historical and current scientific knowledge.

➢ The results of scientific enquiry, the new knowledge and methods used should emerge from different types of investigations and public communication among scientists. In communicating and defending the results of scientific inquiry, arguments must be logical and demonstrate connections between natural phenomenon, investigations, and the historical body of scientific knowledge. In addition, the methods and procedures that scientists used to obtain evidence must be clearly reported to enhance opportunities for further investigation.

Develop the Child's Understanding Based on the Content Standards

1. Biological Sciences

A student who has studied biological sciences up to class 8th should be able to understand what is biology? They should have developed the foundational understanding of biological sciences. When the children reach the class 9th to 12th the understandings of biological sciences will expand by which new concepts emerge on the molecular basis, such as the structure of the DNA molecules, several comprehensive theories, such as the various theories of evolution, genetics, and environmental studies.

The role of a teacher is very crucial, were the role of the teacher is important and it's the teacher who have to decide and make a choice about what he has to teach? How he has to teach? And to what level he has to teach? And which methodology he needs to adapt? This are the things the teacher needs to do; So that, the children are able to develop a proper understanding in biological sciences in a more productive manner. It is essential because of the involvement of molecular biology which would be a guiding factor in the twenty first century as a frontier of science. The children should be able to understand the basic concepts of chemistry and the chemical basis of biological sciences. This would be essential for them to understand some of the practical and ethical implications of humankind's capacity to the manipulation with living organisms.

The children would be able to recognize the word species and based of this they will be able to classify the organisms, a few of them can try to correlate other organisms based on the genus of the organisms. They would be able to exhibit a general understanding about the classification of the organisms and also attempt to do the classification of the organisms when they are presented with the unique organism by studying their characteristics. At times these children also make gross mistakes or blunder classifying some organisms wrongly such as classifying the silverfish, and jelly fish as fishes and classifying penguins and walrus as amphibians as they are seen living on land and water.

Now let us take some examples of a few chapters that are taught in the school from class 9th to 12th. For instance; the content: The Cell: for a child the cell is something that the body of all living things made up of, the cells have specific shape and structure and they perform specific functions. When a child is asked about the structure of the cell the child will respond as; the cell having an outer cell membrane which is known as the plasma membrane. The inner part of the cell consists of cytoplasm which is made up of different molecules that forms the specialized structures that carry out cell functions such as energy production, transport of molecules, disposal of wastes, synthesis of new molecules, storage of genetic information and transmission of genetic information from one generation to the other.

Whenever the child is asked about the cell functions, then they come out that they involve various chemical reactions which are referred to as the biochemical reactions. For instance, the food that is taken by an organism consist of molecules in the form of carbohydrate, proteins and fats, once they are taken by the organism into the cell, then they react with the cell and provide the chemical constituents needed for the synthesis of other molecules. The cell is capable of both break down and synthesis of molecules by specific enzymes with in the cell. The cells are able to store energy.

All the functions performed by the cell are very well regulated by the cell. The regulation of the cellular activity is undertaken by two ways, one by the changes in the activity of the functions performed by the proteins and through the selective expression of individual genes. This enables the cell to respond towards the environment and to control and coordinate cell growth and division.

The child takes the concept that the cell can differentiate and complex multicellular organisms can be formed as a highly organized arrangement of differentiated cells. In the development of these multicellular organisms, the progeny from a single cell form an embryo in which the cells multiply and differentiate to form many specialized cells, tissues and organs that forms the final organism.

The other content matter which I would like to take here and discuss about is –

2. **The Molecular Basis of Heredity**

Now here based on the long spell of education the children had in the lower classes the children would be able to understand that the living organism is able to reproduce its own kind and during the process of reproduction there is transfer of characters from one generation to the other and this is carried out by the Deoxyribonucleic acid or DNA. DNA is the largest polymer formed from the subunits of four kinds of bases, the Adenine, Guanine, Cytosine, and Thymine (which is abbreviated as A, G, C and T respectively). The structural, chemical and the process of replication gives an insight as to how the information is carried and transmitted from one generation to the other. They are carried in a vehicle called as the chromosomes present in the nucleus of the cell and they are transmitted during cell division.

In most of the higher organisms the cells carry a diploid set of chromosomes, for instance, the *Drosophila melanogaster* (fruit fly) carried four pairs of the chromosomes, similarly, the human cell carried 22 pairs of chromosomes, these chromosomes vary in shape and size and they are called as Autosomes and the other one pair of chromosomes is the sex chromosomes. The sex chromosomes are responsible for the transfer of sexual characters for the male it carries the XY chromosomes and for the females it carries XX chromosomes. These sex chromosomes play an important role in the determination of the sexes.

The DNA molecules are subjected to spontaneous sudden changes and this processes is called as mutation and this process takes place at a slow phase or at a low rate. Some of the changes would not make much difference for the organisms, but at times these changes would change the cell and the organism. Mutation in the germ cells would bring out variation in the organisms and at times would change the organisms. The best example is the white eyed fruit fly.

3. Teaching Science and Technology

The basic aim and objective of teaching science and Technology in the school for classes 9th and 12th has two main objectives and those are - to develop within the children the ability to develop technological design; and second is to understand about Science and technology. There are science education standards, the relationship between science and technology is so close that any presentation of science without developing an understanding of technology would portray an inaccurate picture of science.

During the course of solving problems the children try to meet certain criteria within their constraints, they will find ideas and methods of science that they have learnt could be more powerful aids. The children also find that they need to call on other sources of knowledge and skill, such as cost, risk, and benefit analysis, and aspects of critical thinking and creativity. Learning experiences associated with this standard should include examples of technological achievements in which science has played a part and examples where technological advances contributed directly to scientific progress.

The children could understand and use the design model outlined in this standard. Children respond positively to the concrete, practical, out comes orientation of design problems before they are able to engage in the abstract, theoretical nature of many scientific inquiries. In general, a high school student will not be able to understand and distinguish between the role of science and technology. Thus helping them to do so is implied by this standard. This lack of distinction between science and technology further makes the child into more confusion about the perception of science as and when they associate with science and technology with the medical research and use the common phrase "scientific progress". However, they associate technology more commonly with the environmental problems and another common phrase, "technological problems". To relate with the association of science and technology, most of the children, adults and the teachers teaching science have a belief that it is the science that influences technology. This belief is captured by the common and only partially accurate definition "technology is applied Science". Few of the children understand that technology influences science.

The choice of design task and related learning activities is an important and difficult part of addressing this standard. While choosing technological activities of learning a teacher of science will have to bear in mind some of the important issues. For example, he should be able decide whether to involve children in a full or partial design problem; or whether to engage them in meeting a need through technology or in studying the technological work of others. Another issue is how to select a task that brings out the various ways in which science and technology interact, providing a basis for reflection on the nature of technology while learning the science concepts involved.

The children of class 9th and 12th should design and explore a range of concepts including both of those which are immediately familiar at home, school and the community of the children and those wider regional, national or global contexts. This task should be able to tackle the problems so that different design solutions can be implemented by different children. Successful completion of design problems requires that the children meet the criteria while addressing the conflicting constraints where constructions are involved, these might draw on technical skills and understandings developed within the science program, technical and craft skills develop in other school work, or require developing new skills.

The children in the 9th to 12th class should be provided with the task of designing a range of need based projects or problems of different aspects of sciences. A proper designed problem may include the assembly of electronic components to control a sequence of operations or analyzing the future of different athletic shoes to see the criteria and constraints imposed by the sports, human anatomy, and materials. Some tasks should involve science ideas drawn from more than one field of science.

With the introduction of the grading system in the class 9th to 12th class, the children can be used for the designing of several projects or problems that are common in the community and this would help in the speedy improvement of the rural areas. This would also enable the children to improve their skill in problem solving skills and also lead to the development of the rural areas and the community as a whole.

CHAPTER 7

Assessment of Environmental Studies
At The Primary Level

The type of evaluation that we have today in our schools brings about a feeling of insecurity, stress, anxiety and humiliation for most of the school going children. On the other hand, we have teachers who are focussing more on the children to find out what the children have achieved after their effortful teaching in the class; most of the teachers are worried about what the child has acquired from the text book after teaching. In the present system of assessment, we are trying our best to assess the knowledge acquired by the child by means of rote memorization. This type of assessment is not proper and these may also lead to the comparison of the child's performance among the peer groups, and this would create an undesirable competition among the peers' groups in the school. This comparison and the competitions may be for even a half mark difference; the child will be given mental torture by the parents; as a result, the child may even go under depression. Under such conditions, our teachers are not able to do anything but they would come together and think about the problem and find out a solution for such a situation. If these are the outcomes of the examination and evaluation then, what are we looking for when we are trying to assess our children right from the primary classes?

The above mentioned situation is a common thing happening in most of the school in our country. This goes to say that the education system in our country needs to be reviewed completely. Now the question is, what type of assessment stem we are looking for? And under these circumstances if we are trying to modify the assessment patterns then every assessment would be lead to various questions such as those stated below:

What should be our aim of assessment in the schools without putting any hardship to our children? And what should we be assessing in them?

The assessment of our children in schools is an important phenomenon, which is inevitable, and the same is needed mainly to assess our children and to know and understand what our children have achieved in the regular process of class room teaching. We should be aware of the fact; that the assessment of our children in the school is a regular and an important activity, where we are able to understand the performance of the children in the teaching and learning processes. By doing so we are also trying to determine whether or not the required goals of education have been achieved as desired by our teachers in the school. For this we will have to plan a proper assessment method that could be a child friendly one and total care is taken that the children are not put to stress of any kind. The answer to the next part of the question is that we are trying to assess the child's grasping power or the child's mental ability for the acquisition of knowledge of the subject which is been taught to the children by our teacher during their classroom teaching.

Can there be any other means of assessment other than our routine tests and examination?

One of the major objectives of our assessment of the child is mainly to understand whether our child has acquired the required knowledge or whether the child is able to grasp whatever is taught by the teacher in the class room under the teaching and learning processes. At present we have two forms of assessments called as the Formative assessment and the summative assessment. The Formative assessment is usually done by carrying out the assessment of the children after the teacher teaches or completes the teaching of each unit as planned by the teacher. The class test or any other form of examination through which we are able to test or assess the child's performance or we are able to get to know what the child have understood in the regular class room teaching. We should be able to provide multiple choice questions (MCQ) to the children to understand whether the children have understood the basic concepts of the topic which has been taught to them and those which the children are supposed to learn from that particular chapter which is taught and this assessment should be conducted at regular intervals.

Are the present methods of assessments in terms of marks or grades sufficient in the assessment of the child or should we develop any other method of assessment?

The present systems of assessment were we are awarding the marks or grades etc. is not sufficient means of assessment however; the allotment of grades to some extend seems to be better than the allotment of marks. The assessment of the child should be carried out throughout the year. The teacher should be able to evaluate the child on a continuous manner throughout the year. It should be a continuous process. The teacher will have to maintain a register of continuous evaluation of each child and they should keep jotting down the child's behaviour and his performance in academics, child's participation in various class room activities, sports activities and his role in the morning assembly and the child's participation in the co-curricular activities etc. based on the child's activities in the school throughout the year the teacher can prepare a comprehensive report which is called as the continuous and comprehensive evaluation (CCE). We will be going on in details at a later stage in this chapter.

How the information collected by the teacher can helps him in the assessment of the child?

As stated above earlier it has been stated that each and every teacher is supposed to maintain a register of their children in the class. This register should have all the information about each child's information and the activities the children have participated throughout the year. This register will have the teacher's observation about the child's activity in the class, school and at home. His academic performance in the school and the child's participation in various school activities such as the assembly programme, sports, and the child's participation in the school co-curricular activities have to be maintained by the teacher. This would give the general students assessment as a whole. The teacher will be able to assess the child's behaviour his character the child's liking etc. from this report the teacher can very well advice the parent about the child's academic standards and about the child's level of interest in academics or sports or the child's inclination towards any other activity such as the development of the leadership qualities. The child's interest and his future inclination towards his carrier goals and so on.

With less effort, how can the information collected by the teacher about the child's learning can be utilized by the teacher to help in the child's improvement in learning in a better way?

No doubt the question seems to be a difficult one in the Indian context, because most of our teachers have to handle a larger size classes and at the same time, they have to teach two or more classes together and sometimes the teachings have to be carried out in over crowed classes with little or without much facilities made available to them. They also have to handle children coming from different backgrounds, and the teacher will have to interact with children who speak different languages, and sometimes they have to interact with children with special needs also at times. Handling such situations requires more time patience and a greater understanding on the part of the teacher so that they are engaged in education so that the basic aim of education is to educate our children so that they are able to understand the wholeness of life and not merely segments of life like the physical, emotional, mental, psychological or spiritual.

We should have a total integrated outlook of the whole child's life, rather than the compartmentalized outlook. This outlook would bring within the child the sense of creativity and innovative ideas and this shall also make him independent and capable of possessing intelligence without any burden. This shall bring them up as a better human being through education. This type of upbringing through education of the child is not shaped to any particular direction but the development is total and this does not belong to any particular caste or religion or any society but the child develops as a whole human being and not merely as a technician.

Whenever, we are assessing a child then we should be aware of certain facts, such as that they come from different family background. It is essential that we develop a mind set to appreciate differences among them and understand the facts that they will understand things and respond to teaching and learning in different ways. One should also be aware of the fact that the children coming from various sections of the society come to school in class I with a lot of vivid experiences and they come with some kind of knowledge base and vocabulary which mainly depends upon the background they come from. Their knowledge and vocabulary are to be streamlined and filled with proper information and knowledge that needs to be fulfilled and provided by the school. This should be considered as the building of the base for the child's acquisition of new experiences and knowledge, now this would be the base for the child's learning and understanding of the new concepts. Here what I emphasis is that the teacher at the primary level should be able to understand the processes of learning in the child at the primary level. This would help the teacher to determine how the child can be groomed properly and how they can also be assessed during the teaching learning processes. During these processes there are some main points which the teacher need to be borne in mind and these are stated below: -

1. We should always bear in mind that every child has the potential to learn provided they are allowed to do so, but we should also be aware of the fact that each and every child has his or her own pace and their own ways of learning things and understanding them.

2. We should also know that every child has the ability to learn more and more through various activities or by play way method. It is also understood that they are able to do better through peer interactions or if they are allowed to do things themselves.

3. We should always be aware of the fact that learning is a continuous process. We should be aware of the fact that the learning does not take part in the school alone.

The learning should be linked to activities even out of the school and home accordingly the child has to be guided by the teacher.

4. As stated earlier, the above learning should be continuous – this means, that every child is capable of constructing their own knowledge, they don't learn only when the teacher teaches them, but they have the ability to gather information's from their surroundings too, when the child is exposed in his day to day activities this may be a new thing for the child or may be from his previous experiences or whatever the child has learned through his activities in school or at home or anywhere else. Under such conditions the child is able to come out with his own conclusions and the child will develop the ability to make his own understanding in fact every child has a unique way of approach in acquiring his own knowledge.

5. In short; if the primary children are provided with proper opportunity to learn through various experiences, such as play way method, exploration techniques, experimentations and various other techniques such as that of the innovative methods and various other activities would make the child to learn in a better way.

6. As it is known to us that learning among the children is spiral and not linear. Therefore, it is essential that we revisit the concepts again and again at regular intervals; this would help them to understand the concepts in

a better manner. We should be able to understand the facts that the act of learning among the children mainly involves a process of establishing connections of the facts observed or the various experiences that is realised by the child. The learning may be based on the knowledge acquired by the child in the past in the school or from elsewhere.

7. It is important that we are aware of the fact that the children learning mainly depends upon the mistakes and the errors the child commits or makes. The child should be able to realize the mistakes and the errors made by the child and correcting the child. This would help the child to learn the right things.

8. If we are able to go in a systematic way then the children learning would take place in a better and in a holistic manner, therefore; an integrated learning approach would always be better at the primary level.

The Child's Learning and the School Environment

The process of teaching and learning in the school mainly depends upon the school environment. This mainly depends upon the facilities provided by the school to the children, this also depends upon how secure the child is and we are able to keep the child happy by providing a safe environment in the school. To do so the school will have to provide and improve the infrastructure and other facilities; such as providing learning materials, equipment's, teaching aids, space of doing experiments and other activities, space for playing etc. If we are able to provide the required facilities, then the teaching and learning processes among our children can be well achieved provided we are able to promote teaching by play way method or the child centred method of teaching. Here it would be essential to note that the child centred teaching method of assessment would be different and during this assessment one has to assess the child by considering the following facts as stated below:

i. Whenever a teacher is teaching in a child centred class or teaching by play way method, there it is important that the teacher is aware of the fact that he is dealing with the children where there are variety of differences between learners,

ii. Being a teacher it would be his responsibility to cater the needs of each and every child depending upon his pace and the style of the child's learning.

iii. It would be the duty of the teacher to make their class room teaching more flexible and need based, this should be appropriate to the child's age and the child's level of learning.

iv. It would be the duty of the teacher to ensure that the teaching and learning process should be a part of the child's continuous and comprehensive learning.

What is Assessment?

The term "assessment" can be defined in various ways by different individuals or institutions, perhaps with different goals. Here are a few samples of definitions which would give us an insight of the word "Assessment". The Webster Dictionary defines assessment as the action or an instance of assessing appraisal. The assessment in education has been well defined in by Palomba C.A & Banta T.W. in "Assessment Essentials: Planning, Implementing, and Improving Assessment in higher Education". According to them assessment is the systematic basis for making inference about the learning and development of students. It is the process of defining, selecting, designing, collecting, analysing, interpreting and using information to increase students learning and development. San Francisco: Jossey-Bass, 1999, here has stated assessment and defined as – "Assessment is the systematic collection, review, and use of information about education programs under taken for the purpose of improving learning and development."

The definition of assessment of children learning can be made as " the assessment of children learning can be referred to as a participatory, interactive process that, would provide sufficient data/information we need about our children learning, which engages us and other in analysing and using this data/information to confirm and improve our teaching and learning. This also produces evidence about the children learning. The feedback we get would help us to assess and guide us in making our educational system and educational institutional improvements. By this we are able to evaluate whether any changes that is made in our educational system has improved the child's learning and this documents the learning of the children and the efforts made by our teacher's."

The term assessment can also be defined as – "Assessment is the process of gathering and discussing information from multiple and diverse sources in order to develop a deep understanding of what the children know, understand, and can do with their knowledge as a result of their educational experiences; this is the process of subsequent learning."

Assessment can be done at various times throughout a programme and a comprehensive assessment plan should include both formative and summative assessment. This is the point at which the assessment can be carried out in a programme distinguishes by these two categories of assessment.

Formative Assessment

The formative assessment is usually done in the beginning of the programme or during the programme. This could provide us the opportunity for immediate evidence about the children learning their understanding on the subject or the course of their study and the child's knowledge in the course or in that subject at a particular point of time during the programme of study. In most of the schools we have the class room assessment; this is one of the most common methods of formative assessment techniques which are used regularly. The purpose of this assessment technique is to improve the quality of children learning and should not be evaluative or involve in the grading of the children. This can also lead to curricular modifications, when specific courses have not met the children learning outcomes. Classroom assessment can also provide some important programme information's when multiple sections of the courses are taught because this enables the programmes to examine if the learning goals and objectives are met in all sections of the course. It also can improve instructional quality by engaging the faculty in the design and practice of the course goals and objectives and the course impact on the programme.

Summative Assessment

The summative assessment is comprehensive in nature that provides accountability and is used to check the level of learning at the end of the programme. For example, if upon completion of a programme the children will have the knowledge to pass an accreditation test, taking the test would be summative in nature since it is based on the cumulative learning experience. Programme goals and objectives often reflect the cumulative nature of the learning and that takes place in a programme. Thus the programme would conduct summative assessment at the end of the programme to ensure whether the children have met the programme goals and objectives. Attention should be given for using various methods and measures in order to have a comprehensive plan.

Ultimately, the foundation for an assessment plan is to collect summative assessment data and this type of data can stand –alone. Formative assessment data, however, can contribute to a comprehensive assessment plan by enabling faculty to identify particular points in a programme to assess learning and monitor the progress being made towards achieving learner outcomes.

The Assessment and the Right to Education Act 2009

As we are aware of the fact that India is a largest democratic country in this world with the 1.21 crores people (Census Report of India, 2011). But one of the major problems of this country is that 42.1% of people are suffering from inequality in education here (United Nations Development Programme - UNDP, 2014). For this reason, the position of India (India's HDI Rank-135) is too behind than the other developed countries like, U.S.A., Japan, and China in respect to Human Development Index (HDI) (UNDP, 2014). Nearly even after 75 years of independence, India is not able to provide minimum level of education to its all citizen till now. According to the Indian Census Report (2011), only 74.04 % people are literate in India. It means that almost 25.96% people are illiterate in our country India still now. It is in this context and this background, the Right to Education Act (2009) has been taken by the Indian Government which is a historical and significant initiative which has already begins to give pace in the Indian education system since April 1, 2010.

Since independence, Article 45 under the newly framed Constitution stated that the state shall endeavour to provide free and compulsory education to all children until they complete the age of fourteen years within a period of ten years from the commencement of this Constitution. Many decades have passed since independence but we could not achieve the objectives of our constitution to provide free and compulsory education. It was due to this reason the 86th Amendment Act (2000) via Article 21A (Part III) seeks to make free and compulsory education a Fundamental Right for all children in the age group 6-14 years. The amendment also introduced a new article 21 A, which imposes a duty on parents and guardians to provide their children with educational opportunities.

In October, 2003 a first draft of the legislation envisaged in the above Article, viz., Free and Compulsory Education for Children Bill, 2003, was prepared and posted on the website in October, 2003, inviting comments and suggestions from the public at large. In 2004, subsequently, taking into account the suggestions received on this draft, a revised draft of the Bill entitled Free and Compulsory Education Bill, 2004, was prepared. In June, 2005, the CABE (Central Advisory Board of Education) committee drafted the 'Right to Education' Bill and submitted to the Ministry of HRD. MHRD sent it to National Advisory Committee (NAC) where Mrs. Sonia Gandhi is the Chairperson. The National Advisory Committee (NAC) sent the bill to Prime Minister of India for his observation.

The finance committee and planning commission rejected the Bill citing lack of funds and a model bill was sent to states for making necessary arrangements. This was revised and became an Act in August, 2009 but was not notified for roughly seven months. The Right of Children to Free and Compulsory Education Act came into force from April 1, 2010. This was a historic day for the people of India as from that day the Right to Education will be accorded the same legal status as the right to life as provided by Article 21A of the Indian Constitution. Every child in the age group of 6-14 years will be provided eight years of elementary education in an age appropriate classroom in the vicinity of the child's neighbourhood. For the first time in the history of India it is made a right enforceable by pitting in Chapter 3 of the Constitution as Article 21. This entitles children to have the right to education enforced as a fundamental right. Now every child between the ages of 6 to 14 years has the right to free and compulsory education. This is stated as per the 86th Constitution Amendment Act added Article 21A. The government schools shall provide free education to all the children and the schools will be managed by school management committees (SMC). Private schools shall admit at least 25% of the children in their schools without any fee. 'Free' means as removal of any financial barrier by the state that prevents a child from completing eight years of schooling. 'Compulsory' means compulsory admission, attendance and completion of elementary education. 'Compulsion' means as compulsion on the state/local bodies, rather than targeting parents, fundamental duty of parents to send their children to schools.

The Main Basic Provisions of the RTE Act (2009)

In 2009, Indian Government has adopted the 'Right to Education Act' to ensure Free and Compulsory Elementary Education for every child between the age group of 6-14 years by mentioning number of provisions, of which some of them are as under:-

1. It is included in the fundamental rights of Indian constitution in Article 21A inserted by the 86th Amendment in December, 2002. The provisions of the Act came into force from 1st April, 2010.

2. The name of the Act is "The Right of Children to Free and Compulsory Education Act, 2009".

3. It shall extend to the whole of India except the State of Jammu & Kashmir.

4. It is an Act to provide for free and compulsory education to all children of the age of 6- 14 years i.e. from Class I to VIII.

5. Both the Central and State Government will share the financial and other responsibilities.

6. The local authority like, Municipal Corporation, Municipal Council, Zilla Parishad or Nagar Panchayat or Panchayat maintain records of children up to the

age of fourteen years residing within its jurisdiction and ensure admission, attendance and completion of elementary education by every child.

7. The local authority shall ensure admission of children of migrant families.

8. It shall be the duty of every parents or guardian to admit or cause to be admitted his or her child or ward to an elementary education in the neighbourhood school.

9. The private school managements have to take at least 25% of the class strength should belong to the economically weaker sections (EWS) in the neighbourhood at the time of admission in Class-I and provide free and compulsory elementary education till its completion.

10. No capitation fee and screening procedure for admission in elementary classes and no child shall be denied admission if he or she is entitled to take admission according to the provision of the Act.

11. No child admitted in a school shall be held back in any class or expelled from school till the completion of elementary education.

12. No child shall be subjected to physical punishment or mental harassment.

13. A teeacher shall maintain regularity and punctuality in attending the school and complete curriculum within the specified time.

14. The pupil teacher ratio from class I to V shall be 30:1 and from class VI to VIII shall be 35:1.

15. Teacher vacancy in a school shall not exceed 10 percent.

16. No teacher shall be deployed for any non-educational purpose either than the decennial population census duties relating to disaster relief and general election in different purpose.

17. No teacher shall engage himself or herself in private tuition or private teaching activity.

18. No child shall be required to pass any Board examination till completion of elementary education.

19. Minimum numbers of working days/instructional hours in an academic year shall be: 200 working days for Class I to V or 800 instructional hours and 200 working days or 1000 instructional hours for Class VI to VIII.

20. Minimum number of working hours per week for the teachers shall be 45 (forty five) including preparation hours.

21. There shall be a library in each school providing newspapers, magazines and books on all subjects including story books.

22. Play material, games and sports equipment shall be provided to each class as required.

23. National level test shall be conducted like Teacher Eligibility Test (TET) for making eligible the teacher to

teach in elementary classes and maintaining quality in elementary education.

One of the most important features of the Right to Education Act is the introduction of the Continuous and Comprehensive Evaluation System (CCE). It is a mandatory requirement under this act, which needs to be implemented in true spirit by all the states and the union territories up to the elementary schooling level. Here, it becomes essential that the teachers to master the essential class room assessment competencies. As we know that the assessment is an inbuilt component of the teaching and the learning processes. Therefore; it is essential that the teachers should be able to be the masters in the assessment processes in the teaching and learning process. The teacher should not make any mistakes while evaluating the child's progress on the day to day basis during the class room assessment. This means that the teacher should be able to critically analysis and evaluate all the day to day instructional activities that are carried out by the children, teacher and the parents and this could be based on the misinformation about the children success. It is important that the teachers should have a very good knowledge about the subject and good knowledge of assessment and this should be reflected in the teacher's attitude towards the assessment practices done and this will in turn show the teachers competency in assessment. As we understand that the teaching, learning and assessment are complimentary to each other, therefore, there should be a need for incorporating assessment and knowledge as a core subject with due emphasis to the pedagogical content knowledge in the curriculum of the teacher education which were never incorporated in the teacher education.

Evaluation

It was Benjamin S Bloom who recommended the use of evaluation as a part of the instructional process for diagnosis of individual learning, the difficulties for feedback and to the prescribe remedial measures for correcting. It is with these strategies teacher first organized the concepts, skills and learning outcomes, they want the children to learn into smaller instructional units. Here the formative assessment could be used to understand whether the child has learnt well in that subject, and they could also understand what they need to learn in a better way. If the child makes an error the teacher will have to point out first the error, which is the feedback and then this is followed up with further explanation and clarify the subject to ensure the child's understanding. From this feedback and the corrections whatever, information is gained from the formative assessment; the teacher will have a detailed prescription of what more needs to be done for the child to master the subject concepts and to develop the skills from the subject unit which he has studied. This type of correction provided to the child would prevent the child's minor learning difficulties from accumulating and becoming a major learning problem at a later stage for the child. Not only that, this will also give the teacher a practical means to verify, vary and differentiate their instruction and modify their teaching in order to better meet the child's learning needs. This would help many children learn well and master all the important learning goals in each and every unit and shall be able to gain the necessary prerequisite for success in subsequent chapters also (Bloom, Madaus, Hasatings, 1981).

After the children completes the corrective session or the corrective activities in the class period. Then here the Bloom recommended conducting a second formative assessment. This type of parallel assessment should usually cover the same concepts and skills as that of the first assessment, but it should also be composed of slightly different questions from the same concepts and this would serve two important purposes. Firstly, this would help the teacher in verifying the child's performance after the corrective measures under taken by the children were successful or not in helping the children in overcoming of their individual learning difficulties. The second impact is that it offers the children the second chance for success, hence this could be a motivational factor of the children. It is observed that in the first assessment the students perform well then in the first assessment demonstrating that they have mastered the concept and the skills involved in a better way. This process of formative class room assessment combined with the systematic correction method adopted by the teacher will help the children in their learning difficulties. Bloom believed that all the children are provided with an appropriate quality of instruction that is possible under the traditional approaches of teaching and learning. This concept of evaluation is continuous evaluation. The continuous evaluation is a holistic education which aims in encouraging development through the formative procedures not only in its academic subjects but are seen in cross curriculum and co - curricular skills.

Finally, as identified by Benjamin S bloom and other in the year 1956, the comprehensive evaluation can be referred to as the holistic development and assessment of the cognitive affect and psychomotor skills and the behavioural changes. In short; it can be stated that the assessment of the all-round development of the child's personality, would include the assessment of the scholastic and the co-scholastic aspects of the child's growth. As these assessments are carried out in the class room by the teachers continuously in a comprehensive manner; so this type of evaluation is called as Continuous and comprehensive Evaluation and a periodic assessment of the child is also undertaken by the teacher to evaluate the child's academic achievement their skill development and their cognitive growth.

Continuous and Comprehensive Evaluation (CCE)

The term Continuous and Comprehensive Evaluation which is abbreviated as CCE mainly refers to the system of school based evaluation of the children that would cover all aspects of the child's development. This system is mainly designed to assess the children achievement from various perspectives intending eventually so as to eliminate rote learning and cramming. The CCE is mainly based on the principle that the learning is a process which is a continuous activity and this has to be assessed in order to understand how the learner is learning. This means that the evaluation should be treated as an integral part of teaching and learning process through the interrelationship between the expected levels of performance, teaching learning process and assessment.

This concept of CCE is a school based evaluation, this has emerged as the rectification of all the short comings by presenting the results of the assessment of internal and external assessment, this makes both this assessment transparently available for the public to see.

The other features of the continuous and comprehensive evaluation in the school based evaluation is to cover wide range of personality attributes to be just called as comprehensive. This covers the child's academic achievements in school, health status, personal and social qualities, the child's interests, attitudes, values and proficiency in outdoor co-curricular activities. In fact, this will cover up nearly all the scholastic and non-scholastic aspects of the child's growth this would toe to the line of NPE 1986/92.

The other characteristics is that it is continuous this includes periodic evaluation, which is usually under taken through monthly, quarterly, half yearly and finally the annual examination. At the same time, it also attempts to move beyond these to observation of the child's behaviour and attainments on a continual basis.

The evaluation constitutes the third foundation of the concept which basically implies that assessments are to be made with the main purpose of diagnosing the strengths and weaknesses of the child by providing the child with necessary reinforcements by way of remedial or curricular inputs for enabling to have an optimal level of growth among the children in various sectors. One of the most important attitudes of this evaluation scheme is that built in a flexibility for being used without any difficulty in all types of school activity anywhere. The background of the children or the facilities available are no hurdles for its implementation. All the elements in this scheme need not be evaluated. Only a few of these need to be evaluated compulsorily and the rest have to be evaluated only when evidence are available.

The ratings of the non-scholastic aspects are not impressionistic but objective, made on the basis of evidences collected through the anecdotal record forms this needs to be recorded in the final assessment to be recorded in the certificate. This is not to be made by one teacher but it has to be done by a team of at least two for ironing at any element of subjectivity and bias of any single evaluator because of positive or negative biases.

CCE and the Other Types of Assessment

As of now we are confident about the functioning of the CCE, which would mainly focus on the child's progress and their performance with the passage of time. Here there is no need to compare the performance of two or more children. This would help the children to grow in their own pace with proper conceptual clarity with proper understanding of the subject. Assessment is the process in which the information is conveyed for the instructional decision making. The main purpose of assessment is to judge the quality of the performance of the children while learning is going on. Assessment is also to gather the evidences to meet the requirements of evaluation. It is a process through which comparison among various sets of observations are made. Here the evaluation mainly focuses on the levels attained by the child after a certain period of teaching and learning with no interest in why and how that level is attained, this refers to judging the quality of learning. It is also to find out to what extend changes have taken place in the development and in the learning among the children. The assessment is mainly based on the reliable and valid evidence so as to arrive at a precise formulation.

Here the assessment would serve three important purposes:

1. This would inform the decisions taken about the status of learning and to promote greater learning.

2. It would also inform decisions about the accountability of the teachers and

3. This would also reflect on the children own learning based on three purposes: that is the assessment for learning; assessment of learning; and assessment as learning respectively.

These three types of assessment would form the Continuous and comprehensive evaluation. It is important to know that the assessment in learning is usually summative in nature and these three types of assessments are as follows:

> The assessment of learning as stated earlier is summative in nature and it is used to confirm what our children know and what they can do, and to demonstrate themselves whether they have achieved the curriculum outcomes, and to find out whether they have attained the required standards which they are supposed to achieve, and finally, whether the teachers have done their job for which they have been paid for.

> Assessment as learning it is a process of developing and supporting metacognition for the children. The assessment as learning here mainly focus on the role of the children who really act as the critical connector between the assessment and learning, when the children are actively, engaged and they are a critical assessor; and as they make the sense of information, and they relate it to their prior knowledge and the same is used for the new learning. This is a regulatory process of metacognition. This occur mainly when the children monitor their own learning and use their own feedback from this monitoring to make their adjustments, adaptations, and even make major changes which they could understand. Here the teachers are required to help the children to develop, practice and become

comfortable with reflection with a critical analysis of their own learning.

> The assessment for learning is a teacher initiated student – context process and it is integrated with each and every learning activity that is going on in the class room. In this processes of assessment, the teachers would gather information about the child learning using a variety of strategies, tools, techniques and tasks to provide specific and timely feedback about the child's learning. The feedback and the correctiveness which of this assessment would help the child to bridge the gap between the child's current status of knowledge and the desired outcomes of the child.

The Need for Child's Assessment

As a teacher and the educators we must be more concerned about providing the best quality education to our children and at the same time we also want to see that they are properly learning, and it is due to this reason, why we are concerned of learning assessment right from the pre-primary or at the primary level; the reason is that the basic foundations of learning are laid down right at the pre-primary and the primary level, it is here from where the child picks up the basics of education. The basic reasons, why we need to carry out assessment are expressed here below:

i. The main objectives of assessment of the child's learning is to find out what the child has learned, we will be able to understand the various changes that is seen in the child; such as the progress made in the child's behaviour, the child's achievement in different subjects and finally the overall changes that can be seen in the child's personality.

ii. We should be able to identify the child's needs and then accordingly plan our teaching and learning situations in the class in a suitable manner and thus improve the class room teaching environment.

iii. We the teachers should be able to understand the child's pace of learning and understanding, then slowly realize and understand the child's areas of ability and inability to do things and based on this we should also be able to understand what are the child's interest? And then accordingly plan and improve the methodology of teaching in the class.

iv. We as teachers should be able to find out to what extend the curricular expectations and syllabi objectives are achieved by our children.

v. We should be able to provide proper evidences of children's progress so that the same can be communicated to the parents and to the others as and when required.

vi. We should be able to drive away among the children the fear of assessment; and ultimately encourage them to assess themselves.

vii. We should be able to improve and support every child's learning and development, and encourage in them a feeling of confidence and accomplishment.

Education is mainly concerned with the all-round development of the child; and this involves the child's physical, socio – emotional development along with the cognitive development with the full support of the school and their encouragement. Therefore; all aspects of the child's development have to be assessed rather than the child's academic achievement. Here the whole aspect of the child's activities and their performance both inside and outside the class room and the school needs proper assessment. When we are doing so, then we will have to keep these factors in mind which are mentioned below:

a) We should be able to assess the child's learning and his performance in different subject and in different subject areas, so that the child's behaviour and his progress during a specific period of time could be assessed.

b) We should be able to concentrate on different aspects of the child's personality development over a period of time.

c) We need to look into the child's skills, interest, attitude and motivation along with other aspects of the child behaviour and his attitude.

d) It would be essential to observe the child's response to different situations and opportunities both in and out of the school.

It is important that the assessment of learning should be going on, on regular basis along with the teaching and learning process on a continuous manner. We should have a holistic view of the assessment of the teaching and the learning processes, it is important that all the aspects of learning should be given recognition. Here the teacher will have to keep and maintain observations records of the child for a specific period. In other words, the teacher will have to maintain the profile of each and every child present in their class. This profile will help the teacher to reflect and derive the feedback, and based on that the teacher will be able to plan, implement measures that needs to be undertaken for the improvement of the child's learning. The teacher will have to keep an informal observation continuously for a fortnight and then look back and make a quarterly review, discuss and then generally recommend the child for promotion and this process will enhance learning among the children. This type of assessment can be done on –

Daily basis – this can be done by interacting with the children continuously and assessing them both in situations inside and outside the class room.

On periodic basis – this means the assessment can be carried out in every 3-4 months. Here the teacher may check and reflect on the information collected by the teacher during this period.

How Can the Assessments be Made?

The child can be assessed by various steps and means, the process of assessment should be in a cyclic manner and it should be a continuous process. This assessment should have the following steps as given below: -

1. Collection of information's and the evidences from different sources and the methods of collection.

2. There should be a proper recording of all the information's.

3. The information's thus collected should make some sense.

1. **Collection of Information's and the Evidences From Different Sources and Methods of Collection**

We as the teachers, should be aware of the fact that the children learn differently; and it is also known that the learning doesn't take place only in schools but it takes place even out of the schools. Hence it would be essential that we are able to plan the means of assessment properly. As a result, we are able to collect information about the child from various sources which is available, and then we should be able to process the information collected so as to understand the child's learning through their learning experiences and activities.

The main source of information in this case would be the primary teacher. This is because it is they who are involved in the assessment of the child's learning. Here the child plays an important role in the processes of assessment, this is because they themselves play a unique role as they are also involved in the learning processes. The teacher by means of their teaching experiences should be able to develop a better understanding about the children, about the child's requirements through their own experiences and they should be able to design activities to involve the children critically by looking into their own performance and work. This can be done by encouraging the children to select their best pieces of the work and then discuss with the child the reason why they have chosen that piece of work which they have done earlier. Apart from these we should be able to collect information about the children from various other sources also. This can help us in the assessment of the child, and this could be on a continuous basis and this could also throw light on the child's learning behaviour which could also be clear, the teacher should also be able to interact with and get involved with the under mentioned people so that more information about the child can be retrieved and they are –

The parents

The child' friends/peers/and classmates Members of the community.

The following four methods can be used for the assessment of a child:

- Individual assessment: In this assessment the focus is mainly on the child who is performing an activity that is provided to the child. It would be necessary to assess the child how he performs the provided task, and how the child is able to accomplish the provided or assigned task.

- Group Assessment: Here, our main objective is to focus on the child's learning and the progress made by the child in performing the task assigned to him with the objective of completing the same in a group. This method of assessment is important and is also useful in order to understand and assess the social skills, co-operating learning processes and other value related to the other dimensions of the child's behaviour.

- Self-assessment: in this case we are able to assess the child's own ability of learning things and his progress in knowledge acquisition, skills development processes, development of the child's own interests, and the child's attitudes etc.

- Peer assessment: this mainly refers to the process of one child assessing the other children. This assessment can be conducted in pairs or in groups.

In a traditional manner we are used to organize and conduct the paper – pencil test or other tasks that may be in writing or conducts the oral tests or the teacher will present a picture and the child will have to answer the questions based on that picture. Sometimes the teacher is seen conducting small test on the chapter/chapters completed after the end of the unit per month. All these are required for the assessment of the child. We should be concentrating more on the child's ability to develop and promote his or her ability to think; on other hand we should be able to promote in them the sense of thinking, to develop analytical skills, rather than recalling materials from their text book. We should be able to adapt new methods for teaching and assessment in the schools. It is essential that we are able to develop new methods for the assessment of the child and these assessment methods are needed to be used for the understanding of: -

- Learning methods in different subject areas and various aspects of development that can be assessed among the children.

- How the children are given an opportunity so that they are able to respond better to one method as compared to another.

- Each method should contribute in its own way for the teachers understanding of children's method of learning.

By this time as a teacher we might have understood that it is not possible to asses a child with a single tool of assessment. We will have to develop various methods, and for the development of various methods; and for providing and collecting information about the child's behaviour and the child's background and then developing the methods for the assessment of the child's learning and their progress in learning of various areas of development. The teacher will be able to understand and develop the same only with their own experiences. Here the teacher will have to be active and adapt various techniques such are careful observations of the student's activities, listening to them carefully and discussing with them informally along with their friends, peers, parents and other teachers who are teaching them, then assess and review the written work carried out by the child. Then only the teacher will come to the conclusion and they will be able to assess the child.

2. Recording of Infromation Gathered

The most common form of records maintained in every school in our country is about the child's progress in the form of progress card. The progress card mainly contains the grades or the marks obtained by the child in the tests or the examinations conducted by the teacher in the form of class tests or quarterly or half yearly or annual examination. However, these marks and the grades obtained by the children are not sufficient to assess the child's overall achievement, progress and assessment of all the levels of child's learning in a particular subject or subjects. Therefore; it becomes necessary for us to have a proper record of the all the child's activities, assessment date wise and all learning records maintained based on the observations and the performance of the child maintained by the child's teacher.

It is the teacher who can assess the child in a better way about the child's behaviour and the child's learning ability through the teacher's interaction with the children in the class room during the class room teaching. This would provide a better opportunity for the teacher to understand the child in a better way about the child's behaviour and the child's method of learning. The teacher needs to make a day to day observation in an informal way while the teaching and learning process is going on in the class. It is essential here that the teacher will have to maintain a record of all the observations made by the teacher on a day to day basis otherwise, the teacher may forget what he has observed about the child's behaviour and the child's learning behaviour if they are not recorded. Therefore, it is essential that the teachers plan their task well in advance and execute them regularly.

While the teachers make observations, it is essential that the observations are done properly so that we are able to get the proper and a complete picture about the child's behaviour; child's learning methods and the child's progress and achievement in a graded manner. The recording made by the teacher should include in details about the observations made on the child's performance on his assignments project, performance in his class activities, the class should be properly rated on what they do in the class and how they behave with their peers, teachers and others etc. it is also important that the information collected by the teacher is properly understood by the teacher and the teacher is able to draw conclusion on it at a later stage and the same is discussed, encouraged and appreciated by the teacher.

3. Making Sense of the Infromation Collected

The information collected by the teachers can be considered as the available evidences to draw a conclusion and come to an understanding about the child and the child's performance in the teaching – learning processes. Based on these results we are able to draw conclusions about the child's progress in the learning processes. With these available records the teacher is able to understand where the child stands? The teacher is able to take a decision about what needs to be done in order to help the child come out of the ordeal. These are possible only when the teachers with sincerity make a day to day analysis and regularly review the records and then have periodic reflections of the collected information. This information will help the teacher in their regular teaching practices, class room management, and use of materials depending upon the pedagogic aspects and improve on the same for the benefit of the learner. Here we need to have a proper interpretation for the identification of indicators to facilitate this process.

What Are Indicators? Why is it Important?

Indicators are developed to understand the levels of learning in a particular class or the level of education in a particular syllabus at the Primary level. This has been designed based upon the National Curriculum Framework (NCF 2005). These would provide us the broad based frame work of references that the teacher may like to adapt as per the syllabus in general and as per the requirement. The indicators usually help us in number of ways as stated below:-

> ➤ They help us to focus on the understanding of the children's learning on a continuum.

> ➤ It also provides us a reference point for the parents, children and others to understand the progress of every child in a simple way.

> ➤ It would also provide a frame work for the monitoring, learning and reporting about the progress of the child.

Use of Assessment Information

The information's collected about the children can be used by the teacher for –

- **The Reporting and Communicating Feedback on Assessment**

  The assessment of the child carried out by the teacher mainly contains information about the child that needs to be shared for the development of the child. This information's should be transmitted to the child's parents in the form of progress card. This information's collected by the teacher also indicates how much the child has learnt, whether there is any scope of improvement of learning as compared to other children. How effective was the teaching learning processes adapted by the teacher? These also prompt the teacher to use better methods of teaching – learning processes. To achieve these objectives, the process of reporting is essential and this needs to be more communicative, constructive and should be user friendly. This will make the teacher reflect on the information they have based on their day to day observation and these can be used as indicators available in specified areas of learning.

- **Reporting Reflections by the Teacher**

We should be aware of the fact that, for the assessment of the child there should be a proper observation of the child and this is based on the daily and periodic basis. These observations would help in the proper assessment of the child in a proper manner provided the teachers are regular in:-

a) Assessing the portfolio of the children and other records of the children on a periodic basis i.e., quarterly once in every three months.

b) The teachers should be able to review interesting incidents and assess the other aspects of the child's personality properly.

c) The teachers should be able to compare the observations with their earlier records.

d) The teachers should be able to ensure that the same problems should not come up again.

e) The teachers should be able to look at how the problems and difficulties have to been taken care of.

f) The teachers should be able to assess whether the child has improved and find if any weakness still remains, if so, what action needs to be taken in the teaching learning processes for improving them.

We should be aware of the facts that the teacher's reflection is essential and the progress report prepared by the teacher should give the entire mapping of the child's progress. The cumulative report presented by the teacher should give a clear picture of the child's progress over a period of time. Its then only we can properly guide the children's learning in the future and help the child to progress from lower level of understanding and skill acquisition to higher and more complex levels of learning. This will also help the teachers to identify the areas of the child's weakness, difficulties and the teacher will be able to assist the child in mending the gaps. It is through this the teacher will be able to make the required changes in the teaching learning processes. The report generated by the teacher should contain the profile of the child's progress over a specific period of time.

- **Reporting the Feedback on Assessment and Sharing With the Child and the Parents**

  It has been observed that most of the teachers provide informal feedback about our children by ways of activities and the tasks provided to them on the daily basis. The children also correct and try to improve themselves under the supervision of the teacher. Sometimes our children are seen working in groups or in pairs. Once when the work is accomplished, and when the child gets the evaluation report which reflects, what they cannot do and showing their failures or inadequacies, this would de-motivate the children, under these conditions the teacher will have to –

- Discuss with each child about the work done by them. The teacher will have to encourage the child and suggest the nature of implement needs to be done by the child.

- The teachers and the child should jointly find out the type of help the child needs.

- The teacher will have to encourage the child to see the child's profile and help him compare the present work and the past work done by the child.

- The teacher should ensure to provide a positive constructive comment while the child is working or on the work the child has already done.

It becomes the duty of the teacher to encourage the child to compete with themselves rather than looking to others what they are doing.

We should be aware of the fact that the parents are the most interested to know the performance of their child and how the child is doing in the school, what the child is learning in the school and what is the progress of the child over a period of time etc. these needs to be communicated to the parents in an effective manner. The terminology what is written in the progress card such as "can do better", "Good", "bad", "needs improvement", etc. does not mean anything for the parents. At times parents are seen to say that the child is send to school and its teacher's responsibility to see how the child performs. Thus under such circumstances it becomes the duty of the teacher to strive hard to see the child performs better as per the expectations of the parents.

All the information gathered about the child's learning and progress and the feedbacks obtained should be utilised to enrich the ongoing learning and teaching processes. This should help the children to improve and do much better in the learning processes. The assessment cycle should go on and the teacher should be able to assess their own teaching – learning practice properly, the use of TLM, proper planning and providing the children with proper tasks and activities so that the children could be assessed properly based up on the different areas of learning.

- **Reflection by the Teacher for Enriching Child's Learning**

Some of the key questions that could help the teacher's in reflecting and also discussing the child's progress with others can be done by assessing whether our children are involved in various activities and learning optimally. The teacher should be able to understand the different needs of the child and whether the teacher is able to cater to the needs of the children. The teacher will have to assess whether any children is left out and any children is finding difficulty in reaching the teacher. The teacher will have to encourage the child and motivate them individually. The teacher should have the feeling of improving his teaching and learning practice so as to bring their children to the next level of learning and motivate the children towards self - assessment.

Understanding What Our Children Learn in Environmental Studies

As we are aware of the fact that in our country the subject Environmental studies (EVS) is taught in the lower primary classes and this deals with both the social sciences and the science subjects in our schools. Whenever we enter a class room where the teacher is conducting the teaching of environmental studies by the activity based teaching and when the activity based teaching is going on, then we will be able to understand that the children are engaged in their activity for the study of the environmental studies. Here depending upon the activities provided by the teacher to the students, we will be able to see the children making their observations, related to the task provided to them by the teacher which keeps the students engaged in their own exploratory work and sharing their own experiences, they are also seen asking questions to their peers and the teacher and thus gathering information from their peers and other adults and presenting the data collected by them in a survey or by experimentation etc. To understand the purpose of teaching EVS; one has to understand how the syllabus is made and in what way we should assess the children learning of EVS. First of all; let us try to understand how the children learn EVS and what obstacles usually they face in the process of learning EVS. How does their understanding develop in a better way during the process of learning EVS?

How do the Children Learn EVS?

To begin with let us take an example about how our class room teaching is conducted, where the children are engaged in the class room teaching, the children are provided with various activities by the teacher and they are working on it under the supervision of the teacher. Let us assume that the teacher has taken the children out for a field study and the children are exposed to the variety of plants, animals in the surrounding in fact the students are also exposed to the local environment and the teacher explains the interrelationship of the plants and animals in the nature, their food habitats, water bodies and the animal's shelters in details. After coming to the class, the teacher directs the children to recall what they have seen during the field study and jot it down in their note books and try to explain the same in brief. The students are made to sit in smaller groups of four members in one group. The teacher supervises the class room and the children are seen working on the activity provided by the teacher. We will try to analyse and find out whether the children are able to understand the activity and whether they are able to write down the points what they have studied during the field study or the field activity.

It is very important, that the school should be able to provide opportunity for each and every child to learn and happily engage in all the school level activities. For this the teaching and learning processes in the class room must be able to address the needs of all the children based on – cognitive, age appropriate curriculum, conducive and non-threatening environment in the class room. They should have an encouraging school based assessment, thus reporting appropriate practices in the school. If every child is provided with a proper conducive learning environment in the school, then these children would be able to do better and achieve more successfully. We need to visualise the child's learning process in a holistic manner rather than viewing in isolation.

We have all know and have understood that the children learn EVS when they are exposed to real life situations in their surroundings and when they are allowed to construct, and made aware of, appreciates, get sensitized towards various environmental issues, that is prevailing around us. Therefore, it should be understood that the learning of the child always begins from the child's immediate surrounding or the environment starting from the self and the family right from the lower classes, and gradually moving on further to the wider environment issues beyond neighbourhood and to the community at a large.

As per the recommendations of the National Curriculum Framework 2005 (NCF-2005) we have to have an integrated and thematic approach towards the teaching and learning at the primary stage. Thematic approach is always needed when we are teaching EVS in the early classes and then gradually we have to make effort to make our children understand the various issues and the concepts related to natural and social environment from class fifth and onwards. It is also recommended that every effort should be made not to provide direct information, definitions and the descriptions to the children as the child keeps construction of their own knowledge, by using varied teaching and assessment strategies. This requires their own active participation in learning by exposing themselves to diverse experiences acquired through a variety of source within or outside the class room teaching and learning. Based on these varied potential seen among the children then we should be able to carry out assessment simultaneously during the class room teaching and learning and it should be carried out in a natural setting. This would allow us to identify the learning gaps and then based on it we can try to modify our teaching – learning processes to suit the needs of our children. This act would also help in providing timely feedback to our children so as to improve their future learning. It is important that the children should be provided with a variety of learning experience and situations which needs to be presented for the children to participate. This would also ensure that the children participation to observe, express, discuss, question, critical thinking, innovate, improvise, analyse, etc.

Whenever, we are organising the teaching learning of EVS, the following pedagogical principles needs to be kept in mind–

- It should be borne in mind that each and every child is unique, and they have their own strength and weakness. It is also seen that the children learn and progress at different pace and style. It is our observation that some children learn fast by visual aids, were as some children learn by questioning, where as some others learn by observation and by describing it. These children should be given all the opportunity so that these children are exposed to various situations so that they could learn well.

- It is important that all the children need a crucial and are active participation for the construction of their knowledge, using environment as a learning resources. This could provide a better learning for the child and the relate child's knowledge can be correlated with the school knowledge.

- The classroom processes need to be encouraging with the tapping of various sources besides the text book. The teacher will have to be encouraging the learning experiences beyond the four walls of the class room and they should provide the children with a wider perspective of the environment around the child.

- The role of visual aids does play a major role in the teaching and learning of EVS. The readings of visuals by the children would not only provides joy and ethos of written material, but that would also develop crucial thinking and analytical skills but it also can supplement the texts to reduce the content load, picture reading activities in a group with peers could improve social interaction and provides them more opportunities for the construction of knowledge. Care needs to be taken to adapt these visuals for children with visual impairment.

- The learning of EVS must find some suitable ways to sensitise children to the wide differences that exist within our society relating to the gender discrimination, children belonging to the marginalized groups, children with disability, the elders and the sick.

- It is also seen that the children enjoy learning and they will learn more with hands on activities, i.e., by creating objects from locally available materials, draws pictures of their own choice, and involving themselves in arts and craft activities. Children are very happy and they respond with enthusiasm when their creative ventures are appreciated rather than being rejected or are left un-noticed by the elders.

- Based on the observations and the information gathered by the children, each child has the innate potential to learn. Here the child is able to produce their own meaning based on the knowledge the child has acquired earlier. The child's learning is not in an uniform way, the children have a uniform way of thinking and learning and this can become a unique opportunity for them to form the learning resource.

- Since learning and understanding doesn't take place in a linear form, the children's distant memories and their past experiences also add to the process of making some sense of things. To have a meaningful learning it becomes essential for the teacher and the elders to encourage the children to make critical analysis of their prior knowledge or work and then move to the other new concept which needs to be learnt. In short, there would be differences in opinion and varied perspectives would enrich the learning process and this also add quality to what is learnt.

Expectation from EVS Class Room

Here we will have to focus on the overall development of the child that is, the physical, socio- emotional, besides the cognitive needs have to be focused. All these aspects can only be nurtured through a whole range of learning experiences which a child participates in and beyond the school. To assess all these aspects, a comprehensive picture of the child's personality needs to be constructed and this required the information about the child's knowledge, comprehension, skills, values, interests, attitude and motivation in response to various learning situations and opportunities, both in and out of the school. We expect the children learn EVS by developing these skills and abilities. A wide range of suggestive indicators for the learning of EVS has been drawn up so that the teachers can plan learning tasks and activities to fully cover these ranges. The basic objective is to achieve the curriculum expectations/learning outcomes at the end of a particular period of teaching. The learning indicators in EVS are process – oriented. For instance in class III, the EVS curriculum expects learning from the immediate surroundings of the child, where as in class V, curricular expectations need to provide learning related to natural and social environment so that when the child enters class VI, the child would not face any learning gaps in the curriculum transaction of social sciences and science. The learning outcomes would be achieved through a sound and an effective pedagogical process. In EVS learning, the children's response would not be too analysed in right or wrong manner; rather it would provide and promote to put their own point of view about the subject matter. The children are seen to make effort to analyse "why" or "how", they may make mistakes and use their own abilities to correct them also.

The Learning Indicators in EVS Learning

The nature of learning indicators in EVS is mainly process based. For class III to V, these learning indicators are more or less the same. The progression of learning form class III to V can be seen through the complexities seen in the indicators. Now, for proper understanding of the nature of complexities seen in class III to IV, IV to V, suggestive examples are given with each indicators.

1. Observation and reporting – here every effort is made by the child to explore, shares, narrates and draws, picture – reading, makes pictures, collects and records information about by making tables and maps wherever it is required.

2. Discussion – here the child listens, talks, expresses opinion, and tries to discover.

3. Expression – here the child is able to express through gestures body movements, expresses verbally, expresses through drawing writing sculpting, expresses through creative writing.

4. Explanation – here the child gives reasoning, makes logical connections, describes events/situations, formulates one's own reasoning's make simple gestures, thinks critically, and makes logical connections.

5. Classification – the child identifies objects – based on observable features, identifies similarities and differences in objects, sorts/groups objects – based on observable features, compares objects and classifies them based on physical features.

6. Questioning – the child expresses curiosity, asks questions, raises critical questions, frames questions.

7. Analysis – here the child defines situations events, identifies/predicts possible causes of any event/ situation, makes hypothesis and inferences.

8. Experimentation or Hands on activities – here the child is able to improve, makes simple things and performs simple experiments.

9. Concern for Justice and Equality – the child should be concerned towards the sensitivity towards the disadvantaged or people with disability, shows concern for environment.

10. Cooperation – the child takes responsibility and takes initiative, shares and work together with empathy.

The details of the learning indicators and the learning outcomes can be had in details for all the subjects form the book, "Learning Indicators and Learning Outcomes at the

Elementary Stage - 2014" by National Council of Educational Research and Training, New Delhi.

What Is the Role of Teachers in the Assessment of Child Learning?

As we are aware of the fact that the teachers are the main person and it is they who play a pivotal role in the assessment of the child in the class room. The teacher should be active and alert in the class room and should have a proper observational skills and the teacher should keep recording all the observations about the child's activity what the teacher observes in the class room or outside the class room. This would make a proper assessment of the child by the teacher. The teacher should be able to see each and every child as a person; the teacher should be able to gather further information about the child from other teachers and they should be able to collect information about the child from the child's parents too.

After collection of all the information's from all the available sources then the teacher is aware of the child's various dimensions of the child's prior learning i.e., his style of learning, his interests, needs and preferences for his learning etc. now by identifying the socio – affective and psychomotor characteristics, then the children should be provided with a clear and understandable version of the learning goals right from the beginning of the teaching and learning processes. After indentifying and providing success criteria of these learning goals shall be used by the teachers for their assessment. It is important that the children are made to reflect on their own learning strength and weaknesses and to evaluate learning according to the criteria for success. It's important that the children are provided with timely descriptive and constructive feedback based on the identified success criteria and corrective to improve current as well as further learning. There should be an increase in variations in teaching and that would be based on the needs of the learners; for this the teacher should have a thorough knowledge of the content and the pedagogical knowledge is also essential. The teacher must be able to understand his role as a scaffolder and should be able to close the gap between where they are now and where they want to reach.

It is important for the teacher to engage the children in the learning activity and in the assessment processes so that they reach the achievement targets so that the children are able to make them responsible for their own learning. The teacher should be able to select a proper appropriate assessment method by considering the child's background, his interest, skills and the child's availability in the school premises. The teacher should be able to make use of the available multiple sources of information about the child and use them in the assessment of the learning in the class room and make the child's evaluation more reliable, valid and much more fair. In this case the teacher should be more skilled so that he may draw proper inferences and make proper reporting in the progress card of the child. This is only possible if the teacher is well versed with the assessment tools, the teacher will have to know the various strategies and techniques for the analysing and interpretation of various success criteria used in the for learning, this may lead quality assessment of the educational processes. Finally, in short; the teachers should have to follow the meta-cognitive strategies and a constructive approach to make assessment as a process oriented performance based on the assessing of the child's ability based on the set criteria.

Finally, in conclusion, I have to state that the introduction of the Continuous and Comprehensive Evaluation is a boon for the education system, the main purpose of introducing the same is to do away with the rote learning. Implementation of the CCE in the true sense in schools needs and requires that the teachers are thoroughly aware of the CCE and the class room assessment methods. As stated earlier that the teacher will have to treat all the children as their own child and then carry out the assessment. What is needed is that the teacher with a proper attitude and awareness about the skills to practice it effectively. The teacher should be aware of the facts that how the children learn and how this learning can be assessed, this aspect should be a major part of the teacher's education and the teacher's professional developmental program. The training should be linked to actual experiences in the class room assessment and interpreting the development of the child's competence.

Lastly, as we know that the assessment of the child in the learning and the teaching process is more important and the child should be assessed based upon the performance made by the child in the class test or exams or the various activities carried out by the teacher in the school. The teacher will have to maintain a record of the child's performance in a proper way so that the child's behaviour can be also assessed. These should be well assessed based upon the learning outcomes and the learning indicators as the standard maintained and lay down by the studies conducted by the various agencies in the field of educational assessment. For instance, we have the learning Indicators and Learning Outcomes at Elementary stage as maintained by the NCERT in our country. However; we cannot go word to word as per that book because there could be variations in the observations of the teacher on the child's performance. These needs to be assessed properly by the teacher and it's the teacher who is required to draw inferences which needs to be taken by the teacher as we are assessing the students and this should be done in a proper way without harming the sentiments and the interest of the students so that the students don't lose interest on education and towards the learning processes but they should be able to generate keen interest towards education as it is a lifelong process.

CHAPTER 8

Communication Skills of English Language at the Primary Level

In our country, the teachers are facing many challenges, out of these one of the primary challenge which our teacher face is teaching of English language at the primary level. Educational guidance is required for our teachers at every stage of Education, namely the Pre-primary, Primary, middle school, high school, higher secondary, university and at the professional level.

As stated in the previous chapters it is been observed that when the children come to school from preprimary to Primary level, they feel it difficult to comprehend the ways of learning skills in the school atmosphere, social pressures and the social expectations does also plays an important role in determining habits of obedience that should be established and the consistent discipline needs to be maintained. The teachers goal is to let the children know about what behaviour is approved and what is disapproved and then to motivate them to behave in accordance with their school standards.

These children usually take some time to get themselves acclimatized, and adjusted with the new school environment. It would take some time for the teacher also to set these children and mould them and bring them to the school set up and routine so that these children are able to settle down and come to the main stream of education in the new school environment. It is important to note that the children who seeks admissions and comes to our schools in India; do come from various background and with different dialects of languages spoken in our country, this is because India is a multi-linguistic country.

The medium of teaching may vary in various schools in our country. It has been seen that the parents are more eager to admit their children in an English medium school. This trend has been seen even in the rural parts of the country. Whether the child is admitted in the English medium or in the Hindi medium or in any other local language medium of teaching in schools. The problem faced by the teachers teaching any language at the primary level do face the same problems of motivating the children and making them adjusted to the new school environment.

Let me take the example of the children who are admitted in an English medium school or into a Hindi medium school. For instance, let us take the example of the children who seek admission in Kendriya Vidyalayas, where the medium of instruction is both in Hindi and English, this would certainly bring in these children a lot of confusion in their minds and at times the child does get themselves scared and at times; we have children who does not like to come to school. When the children are under such a psychological state of mind; even then, I have to appreciate our primary teachers in KVS, who try to mould these children and bring them to the standard of the KVS by making the children to shun their psychological fears. These children are moulded in such a way that they would excel in these languages, but at the same time these children are also seen to do well in various ways in their presentation on various subjects and do well in any of these languages by means of presenting things in writing, reading, speech etc.

Now as we are all totally depending upon science and technology for the development of this nation; however; we cannot forgo the teaching of English language. We should understand that the English language is an international language and the knowledge of English is needed for our children to excel well in science and technology to compete with the other developed nations. Further, I have to state that when there is a great demand for our children who are highly educated with good technical skills in the world's international work market, then the knowledge of English is very essential for our children to grab that opportunity. Therefore, the teaching of English language becomes a very important for our children right from the pre-primary stage and it becomes our prime duty to see that our children gets the best English language teaching right from the pre-primary classes.

Learning of language; may it be any language, this would provide excitement, enjoyment and a challenge for the children and the teachers who help them to create enthusiastic learners; it is the teachers who would help them to develop positive attitudes towards any language learning throughout their life. The natural links between the language and the other areas of the subject curriculum could enhance the overall teaching and learning experiences. The skills, knowledge and understanding gained by the children could make a major contribution to the development of children's oral ability and literacy skills and it is through this the children are able to understand their own culture and at the same time they are able to understand the culture of the others in the society. Further, I have to state that it is this language which also provides an individual identity for the child and his identity as a person in his community. The child's ability and interest to learn other languages can do a great deal in shaping our children's ideas, thus giving them a new perspective on their own language.

Language teaching has always had a central place in primary education and in the primary curriculum since independence of our nation. India is a multilingual country with numerous languages and dialects spoken and written. There are about 1652 languages/dialects belonging to five different language families in our country. There are 22 schedule languages mentioned in the 8th Schedule of the Constitution. Over 87 languages are used in the print media and 71 languages are used in the audio media. But only 47 languages are used in the media of instruction in schools across the country in which English is one of them. English is also associated as an official language at the national level.

English is a language which is used in India for more than two and a half centuries; but in spite of this only a few people are able to speak English, this is because English is a language which is not spoken by many people in this country, even though English is a language which has a major links between the national and the international level and it is also a language which is commonly used in the offices, business, industries, and for the making of the professionals, like the doctors, engineers and in the field of basic and applied research especially in science and technology. It is due to this reason the teaching of English has gained greater importance today, and the teaching of English has become more important and it is due to this reason English language is introduced in our educational system right from the school level. Not only that; the people even in the rural areas also have a desire to educate their children through the English medium rather than any other language.

During the census of 2001 it was found that about 2.3 lakh Indians used English language as their primary language; and about 86 million listed English as their second language and other 39 million as their third language, thus making a total of English speakers in the country as over 125million. This figure might have increased further after the 2001 census. This statistic gives us an insight about the growing popularity of the English language in our country.

Development of English language in India – An Historical Account

English language made its first appearance in our country with the advent of the East India Company, who entered the country for trade but slowly took control of the countries administration. The missionary schools which were started by the British way back in the 1800s started teaching English as a language in their schools. The Lord Macaulay's Minutes of Indian Education (1835) advocated strongly the use of English as it felt that "Indians cannot be educated by means of their mother tongue. English is the language". He also envisaged that English would be the language of commerce, politics and judiciary.

Lord Macaulay's minute of education dated 2nd February 1835 was approved by the then Governor General of India, William Bentick on the 7th March 1835, and it became the corner stone of the British India Educational Policy. Thus English became a language of the affluent in the Indian Sub-continent as a result of this policy alone the bureaucracy thus opened opportunities for those Indians knowing English.

English Language After Independence

It is important to know that education plays an important role in the development of any nation, so is it with our country. Since independence we have number of Educational Commissions and Committees which was set up by the Government of India after independence and they have given their recommendations and suggestions on various aspects on education and about the teaching of English language. The official language Commission which was formed by the Government of India under the Chairmanship of B.G. Kher recommended seven years of English language teaching in schools (Kher 1957). The report of Education Commission (1964 -66) recommended the teaching of English after the primary level. The conference conducted on the teaching of English in the primary schools suggested changes in the thinking about the proper age and level for teaching English in schools (Gokak, 1963). The Kunzru committee (1959) recommended English as a second language, but the Central Advisory Board of Secondary Education (CABE) proposed the 3 –language formula and the same was approved by the conference of the Chief Minister held in 1961 and that was accepted as a part of the educational policy. Thus English was to become one of the three languages to be taught at the upper primary level. Later most of the states modified this policy and decided to introduce English at the primary level itself. Later several states adopted the policy of discontinuing the teaching of English at the primary level in the government schools. Later when English became a major language to be used in scientific research, information technology and commerce sector, then there was a significant change in the public opinion in favour of English and so there is a revival of English teaching at the primary level in nearly all the states.

Language learning doesn't mean acquiring the skills of listening, speaking, reading and writing but it also consists of developing proper communication skills and other competencies among the children is also important.

The Sarva Shiksha Abhiyan (SSA) launched by the Government of India as a flagship programme for providing free and compulsory education to children of 6 -14 years of age it has also suggested that the teaching of English may also be recommended for teaching and learning right from the lower class one onwards, it is also further suggested to give English a greater importance at the school level.

The National Knowledge Commission (2007) has made a recommendation that time has come to teach English as a language in the schools, an early action in this direction would help us to build an inclusive society and transform India once again in to a "Knowledgeable society", which it was a few decades ago. It was also recommended that the English teaching should start right from class one so that the child after acquiring 12 years of schooling the learner will have access to higher education and also get equal access to employment opportunities.

A General View about Language teaching at the Primary Level

When we are talking about language teaching at the primary level then it is essential that we also talk about the universal human language which makes some sense for making and communicating various means of communication in art, music, literature and drama. It is important to understand that language is not simply a conduit of thought, but it is a vehicle on which we are able to place our thoughts and our expressions down the lines to somebody else. In fact, we are able to create and recreate our thoughts and express the same to others. Thus, here the language should be a means for the purpose of creation and recreation. The mental processes that makes creativity possible is nothing but imagination and it is through this imagination lies the future which one can envisaged. It is this imagination which is the explorer of many new possibilities, it is an engine of progress in art, literature, science, business, even our personal relationships, etc., therefore, imagination is very important. This imagination is critical and very important for leading a very rich life. Its cultivation should not become a luxury as the emphasis would shift on to paper work, targets and an increasing workload.

Language teaching is something which has a number of dimensions, and these mainly includes the development of oral expression, development of written skills, literature, and creativity. All these are the parts of a language curriculum which is commonly seen in our schools. Our aim of language teaching in the primary schools should be to encourage and assist our children to use the language, whatever they learn, should be used by the children fluently and the pupil should be able to express their ideas freely and very clearly.

We should be able to encourage and teach our children to read their texts or books both for information and for pleasure.

There are several evidence which shows that the early childhood learning among the children is mainly based upon the sensory experiences. There are also several evidences which shows that the children begin to form concepts at an early stage of their life and this is mainly based on a wide variety and wide range of interactive sensory experiences. The rate and extend of children's learning in the early years is much greater than that of any other period in their life. One of the most unique features in the range of learning is the extraordinary amount of language a child learns or acquires during the first three and a half to four years of age. By the time the child reaches this age, the child will have not only acquired an impressive vocabulary but most of the children will have also mastered the grammar and the syntax of the mother's language. However; the child will still make grammatical mistakes.

Now the important question is how is the children able to learn so much of the mother tongue in such a short time has been worked out by the psychologists, linguists and the educationalist. This has led to number of theories which I shall not touch here now. However, the mastery of languages what the child acquire by the age of three and a half years to four years cannot be explained in terms of any imitation or teaching, whether formal or informal, however, both imitation and teaching does play an important role in the mastery of languages by the children.

There is another important factor that needs to be taken into account while considering the language learning. The major role of language and its basic function is of communication, either with oneself or, more importantly, with others. The main use of language is for a social act, this mainly involves listening and communicating with oneself, communicating some information, or an idea, or an opinion to others, or responding to the ideas, opinions or information received from others. This interactive context and the function of languages is of a greater significance both in learning and in the language learning, and particularly so on mainly in the early years. The ability of the young child to form the concepts prior to any significant degree of language acquisition has been already referred to. As the concept of language develops, the child is able to acquire the means of using symbols to represent concepts. The accuracy and comprehensiveness of the concept will, of course, depend on the broader experience, but the symbol can now represent a variety of characteristics and dimensions that can be add up to the concept. However, the concept formation develops with the sensory experiences, but as language is acquired by the child then the child is no longer dependent solely on sensory experience for further concept development.

The experience developed by the child now plays an important and a continuing role in concept formation, but as the child matures, then the language will not only play a very important role, but it will afford the child's ability in expanding the existing concepts acquired but it and will help the child in the developing of new concepts that will not only outstrip the capacity of direct experience but adds to the child's knowledge exponentially. Words gain new connotations, and are linked with other words, which are combined to form new concepts, and this help to make abstraction more manageable and communicable. The language use and the language interaction are crucial in this process, not just in the early years but throughout the child's experience in the primary school. The circuitry in the child's brain would allow them to learn the grammar of their parents' language, and this also helps in language development that cannot occur unless it is activated through language use and language interaction. Hence, the child's experiences of language interaction in their home and in the school are important and the quality of that language interaction will have far-reaching effects in the terms of both languages learning and learning in generally.

The most important feature of language learning is the development of literary. The ability of the child to read and comprehend text is the center to success in current and future education and also to develop an ability to function in the modern society. Several surveys were carried out worldwide and this have raised questions in relation to the levels of literacy achieved by various educational system in the world, However, it is important to bear in mind that all of these studies would refer to the attainments of literacy among the children, who have experienced approaches to the teaching of emergent reading and reading that were prior to the introduction of the Primary School Curriculum. The main features of the English language curriculum are believed to give support for the acquisition of literacy, the comprehension of text, and how children should respond to their text.

In the early 1960s, Basil Bernstein, a British sociologist, expressed the relationship between school performance and socio-economic background of the child; this could be explained in terms of variations in the forms of language found in different social classes. He is best known for coining the terms 'elaborated code' and 'restricted code' this was in relation to the way language is used and structured in different social groups. According to Bernstein's view children from the working class homes use a restricted code of language which is likely to frame what is being said in such a way that listeners must be aware of, or share, the physical situations of the speakers in order to understand what they mean. On the contrast, the children from better off homes tend to use an elaborated code, which uses language in a way in which the thing being referred to is first established verbally. Bernstein believed that children who are fluent in the elaborate code come to school prepared for the linguistic demands they will encounter in the school while children who use the restricted code are likely to find learning relatively difficult. Bernstein's theory was embraced by educators and politicians in the USA and they used as a stimulus for political action to provide educational opportunities for children coming from poor homes.

One of the possible explanation for the link between social background and the school performance can be expressed in term of ease of communication between teachers and the children from different backgrounds. Brown and her colleagues (1994) conducted an extensive investigation of communication between the Scottish school children and their teachers. Based on this Scottish research is a distinction between what their searchers' term 'chat' and 'information giving speech'. These researchers studied nearly 500 children from the age of fourteen-to-seventeen-year-old school going children, among these 300 children were judged by their schools whom were to be in the lower third of their year in academic ability. The main findings of the study were that academically less able children were weak at using speech for information-giving purposes. It was discovered that these children were usually incapable of providing coherent, comprehensive, informative narrations. Even when the Language teacher in the Primary School asked the children to tell the researcher about familiar events the children were frequently uninformative and they felt it difficult to understand. But when the children were observed chatting to each other in pairs the children were talkative, and they were very often witty, and seemed to suffer with no problems of communications. It is worth noting that the findings in relation to 'chat' were consistent with

Chomsky's theory of the innateness of language acquisition whilst the findings on 'information giving speech highlighted the difficulties caused by the differences between children's everyday experience of language and the use of language in schools.

Brown and her colleagues did more than their observation and they designed an intervention programme which they felt that this would help children develop their crucial information giving skills. The programme contained communication games in which one child had to tell to another child how to perform a task. Other tasks in the programme involved creating narratives.

As a follow up of their studies of the programme, it was found that the children remembered what they had learned, and they were able to generalize what they had learned in one task to improve their performances in another. One of the most significant finding was that the children who played the role of listeners were significantly more articulate and informative when it came to their turn to play as the role of speaker; than were the children who were first asked to act as speakers. This experiment carried out suggests that listening, at least in some contexts, it is a powerful tool for learning, here the children learn how to talk informatively is an exclusive experience as a speaker.

This apparent success of this intervention also suggests that the children can be helped to become more articulate and fluent in their powers of self-expression. It further, suggests that the children can demonstrate their innate language ability in relaxed conversation whilst facing considerable difficulties in trying to explain themselves or instruct others. There is also evidence that the information-giving skills which seem to be essential for academic success do not come about naturally or inevitably; they may demand the specific types of experience which were provided by Brown and her colleagues for the children in the intervention programme.

There has been considerable relevance for the teaching of English language in primary schools. It is important that children develop linguistic skills that are appropriate, not just to the social life of the community outside the school, but that will enable the children to benefit fully from the education system. In this context, the relationship between the linguistic abilities of the children from disadvantaged backgrounds and their success or otherwise in the school system is highly relevant. Although the English curriculum incorporates language activities such as those used by Brown and her colleagues, it may be relevant, in the process of reviewing the curriculum, to address specifically the language learning needs of children from disadvantaged backgrounds.

English Language Teaching and the role of NCERT

When we are writing about education in India, then we cannot ignore the role of NCERT in our Indian Education system. NECRT was first founded and established in the year 1961 as an autonomous organization by the Government of India to assist and advice the central and the state Government on the policies and the programmes for qualitative improvement in school education in our country. The NCERT also carries out Educational Research in our country, and it is also responsible for the framing of the curriculum and its implementation in our schools run by the Central Government and the State Government. This is the only organization in our country, which is involved in the planning and the implementation of the educational curriculum in our country and it also evaluates the outcomes of its implementation in our country.

When we are talking about English language teaching in our country, then we cannot forget the role of NCERT in English language teaching in India. Here, in India the teaching and learning of English language what we have today is mainly characterized into two, on one hand, we have a diversity of schools and a linguistic environmental supportive system of English acquisition, and on the other hand, we are having a systematically pervasive classroom procedure of teaching English in with the teacher uses a text book for the children's success in an examination, modulated by a teacher who believes in influencing the child to a varying degree by providing them inputs from the English language teaching as a profession.

The teaching of English in most of the English medium private schools may differ in the learning opportunities they offer, and this can be reflected in the differential language attainment. Studies carried out by Nag-Arulmani (2005), comes out that the children in these schools having the class libraries can read better than those in schools where reading is restricted to monotonous texts, and frequent routine tests of spelling list. Another study carried out by Mathew (1997) in a curriculum implemented study, in CBSE affiliated schools differ in the "culture" arising from "the type of Management, funding, geographical location, salary structure, teacher motivation, and their competence, and the type of children they cater for and the type of parents".

Traditionally the English language was taught by the grammar translation method. In the late 1950s structurally graded syllabus was introduced as a major innovation into the state system for the teaching of English language (Prabhu 1987). The main objective was that the teaching of language could be systematized by proper planning its inputs just as the teaching of other subjects like arithmetic or other science subjects.

Based in the practices in the class room led to the fragmentation and trivialization of thoughts by breaking up language in two ways, first into structures and into skills. These forms mainly focused on the teaching of language aggravated the gap between the learner's "Linguistic age" and "mental age" to the point where the mind could no longer be engaged.

As per the NCERT the goal for the language curriculum can aim for a cohesive curriculum policy based on guiding principles for language teaching and acquisition, this allows for a variety of implementations suitable to local needs and resources, and which provides an illustrative model for use.

English Curriculum at the Primary Level

Whenever, we are framing the English curriculum then it is essential that the same should be mainly based on two fundamental principles and they are:

1. Language is divisible,

2. The children not only learn English but they learn through language,

The language curriculum should always be a framed or structured in such a way that it reflects the above two principles. In order to emphasis on the first principle, oral language, reading and writing are inextricably linked to language use and language learning. The main divisions of the curriculum are the different strands, and these are not the above mentioned three skills i.e., oral language, reading and writing but there are four more wider language learning goals which are mentioned here below.

1. Receptiveness to the language;

2. Developing Competence and confidence in using the language;

3. Developing cognitive abilities through language; and

4. The emotional and imaginative development through language.

Among these strands of the curriculum there are three strand units which is mainly based on the activity in oral language, reading and writing. In this way, each of the strands would provide an integrated language experience for the child in which the three skills would interact with one another. The second principle is also reflected in the organization of the strands. Broadly speaking the first two strands, such as Receptiveness to language and developing competence and confidence in using the language, are mainly directed for the child's language learning. The other two strands, developing cognitive abilities through language and the emotional and imaginative development through language, are mainly concerned with stimulating and motivation of the child's learning through their language learning. However, these are the centrality of the first principle and that is due to the complexity of language and the process of language learning, this is seen in both learning the language and learning through language are of greater necessity, and these are addressed in by all the strands. However; these strands represent the four broad goals of the curriculum and these are central to its realization as far as the language teaching programme is concerned.

Motivating children to use oral language is a very crucial element of experience in each of the strands and at every level. This has a crucial role not only because both reading and writing activities are also a part of the English curriculum and it is also a teaching strategy in every curricular area. Providing too much oral language work will have to be accomplished in these two contexts; however; it is envisaged that the teacher will also have to devote discreet time to oral language in mediating the English curriculum.

A similar approach to reading is also espoused by the curriculum and it reflects the most successful international theory and practice. The development of phonological and phonemic awareness is at the core of the emergent reading phase. These can be addressed through extensive oral language activity, involving rhymes, rhythmic activities, language games, and onset and rime. These activities will have to take place in the context of a print- rich environment, of which the library corner in the class room will have to be a central feature, the experience of a collaborative reading with the teacher using large-format books and language experience materials, and the provision of consistent opportunities to browse and read books in the library corner.

From the beginning the child should be encouraged to read for the understanding of the meaning and to respond to the text in a variety of ways. The children should also be encouraged to a wide variety of material that should include narrative, informational and representative texts. Arising from the importance given to reading for meaning, at the same time greater stress should be laid on the development of comprehension skills, starting from the basic comprehension skills at first; and later effort should be to achieve higher comprehension skills also.

A systematic approach to writing in the curriculum is mainly based on the principle that the children learn to write through writing. They should be encouraged to write on a wide range of topics, for different audiences, and in a variety of genres. The main objective of this approach starts right from the early years and it should be to develop the process of writing, editing and redrafting. This would enable the child to draft a piece of writing and then discuss it with the teacher. Through this conferencing process, as the curriculum terms it, the teacher will, by suggestion, and encouragement, would help the children to improve their expressiveness and accuracy of their writing, with this event the main aim is to enable the children to become an independent writer who could recognize different registers of language and their appropriate use. It is principally through this writing process, the child's mastery of grammar, punctuation and spellings are also developed and improved to a greater extend.

Organizing Time for Oral Language Teaching

By this point we are aware of the fact that the oral language teaching would help in the development of language skills among the children. This will also enable the children to ask questions, help them to reflect their activities, help them for the use of phone, and help them to take part in conversation and convince people towards them; in fact, here the children are able to understand and grasp the basic skills of conversation which they are supposed to develop. It is more essential to ensure that more and more oral language activity is taking place in the class room as per the curriculum needs; one should be able to see that the oral language teaching is deeply embedded in the teaching strategies in every curriculum area. The teachers should be able to understand and see that these forms of oral language activity are a very much an important part of the English language programme.

A popular approach in the planning for an oral language is the use of various themes and topics that can be integrated with two or more other subjects too; such as mathematics, geography, history and science. It is also observed that the value of oral language activity is also seen to develop children's cognitive abilities while dealing with various topics and themes, and that there was a positive relationship between discussion and learning. It is also stressed that planning should not be so rigid and inflexible so as to inhibit the teacher in using various opportunities for oral language activities as these should arise spontaneously in the course of classroom activity.

Teachers do have several problems in planning discrete time for oral language activity, and preference has been indicated, to plan its integration with other subjects; but, although this does not strictly involve the planning of discrete time for oral language activity, it is indicative of planning for the use of oral language. This discrete time planning for the oral language activity can be done in ten or fifteen minute slots at least once or twice a week in the class room teaching.

A number of various other issues may also rise in relation to oral language activity in the classroom. It has been seen that the older children usually tend to dominate discussions session, even the teachers in some single-class situations shall also encountered similar situations in relation with the children who were more confident and articulates than others children. We have only one solution and that is by the use of groups of like aged children to discuss topics relevant to them. The problem of class size is also one of the factors which seem to be acting as an inhibiting factor in the management of the oral language activities. Young children, especially those who have language skills below the level of many of their peers and needed considerable vocabulary enrichment work to enable them to benefit fully from the approach of oral language as per the curriculum. The teachers may find it difficulty in assessing oral language development, in assessing the progress and attainment, and in assessing the effectiveness of the methods they were using. A number of approaches to oral language assessment were mentioned. These included the use of audio and video tapes, and one-to-one sessions between teacher and child every three weeks or so.

Encouraging Children to Respond Towards the Text

After trying to implement all the new approach of teaching language, it's now time for the teachers to find out how much the children have achieved by the use of all these new approach of reading. Experimentation carried out in Ireland showed an increase in the amount of children reading in the school, greater varieties of texts they were reading, they were found to be encouraged to respond to their text by various ways, the extent to which school and class libraries are being used was encouraging, and the willingness of teachers to use discrimination in choosing reading materials. Use of the novel seems to be widespread in schools. In some schools it is used as the principal reading material in the class, but more commonly it is used in conjunction with a variety of other reading materials. Approaches to its use are varied and imaginative. In some cases, particularly in the junior classes, the teacher reads the novel aloud and children respond to it. In other cases, children read in groups and discuss what they have read. In other cases, still, children read novels individually and the teacher encourages response in a variety of ways.

A notable point of consensus which was seen is the commercially-produced reading materials were widely used; it was seen that the teachers were consistently supplementing them with other reading materials of their own choice, in particular with library books. In certain cases, dissatisfaction with the materials for the infant classes were expressed. Some of the teachers preferred creating their own reading material for their children by encouraging them to produce stories of their own, which were then used for reading. In fact, it was seen that the teachers were moving away from the class reader to core reader. Some teachers supplement it with other reading material. It was felt that the class reader was still useful in meeting the reading needs of weak reader's effort was made to see that they could feel that they could finish at least one book reading in a year so that they were encouraged.

It was evident from the above study that the teachers are encouraging children to respond to text more than they did before the curriculum began to be implemented. This is because of the children's reading habits developed in school, but it is also an indication of how much the teacher has embraced the new approaches of language learning. However, response is largely encouraged through the more traditional forms of oral language, writing and art. There was no indication of encouraging children to respond in other methods which is the more imaginative ways of activity such as dance, drama and mime. In fact, the teachers seem to find it easier to get children to respond to fiction rather than informational text. This was because children could relate fiction more easily to their own experiences. Although it was recognized that the importance of developing children's higher comprehension skills, a very little evidence emerged from the discussions that these were being addressed satisfactorily. Reference was made to the importance of oral language work and the use of discussion in relation to developing comprehension skills. Some stressed the use of discussion in developing comprehension skills whereas other stressed on oral language activity before reading the text. Several participants recognized that more was expected of teachers in addressing the development of comprehension skills but, by and large, there were content to rely on commercially-produced materials to teach them. However, there seemed a misconception about the relationship between response to text and comprehension.

Teaching Children About Writing, Editing and Redrafting

Several studies were carried out in Dublin which also suggests that the children were encouraged to write and they also enjoyed writing right from the primary school. This approach towards the teaching of writing was supported by the primary school curriculum. This is sometime called the process writing, which also emphasized the process and importance of teaching the children how to write though the process of writing. This can be affected through a process of writing, editing and redrafting. This process would envisage children in writing a piece which would be followed with an initial discussion involving the teacher and the class, the production of the first draft. Now having a 'conference' with the teacher about this first draft, and then redrafting the same piece in a way that will reflect that process of conferencing. This process may or may not be repeated for one or more times, depending up on the nature, and the purpose and it also depends upon the audience.

Here it is important to understand that the discussion that takes place indicates the teacher's commitment to, and the acceptance of, this approach to the writing is mixed. Some participants feel that it makes the children very excited about the process of writing, so that they put much of their time and thought into their writing, and they took a lot more trouble for their final presentation of their writing. Whereas others did have considerable reservations about it, and it was evident that these reservations were inhibiting teachers from committing themselves fully to this approach of writing. It has been seen that a number of participants were making genuine and reasonable attempts to follow the approach which is outlined in the curriculum and its guidelines. However, a number of misconceptions as to the nature of the approach were also evident. Chief among these was a faulty understanding of the purpose of the elements of conferencing and redrafting in the process.

Here the curriculum envisages that these were being principally directed towards improving children's powers of expression in written language. The discussions, however, make it abundantly clear that the participants' conception of the purpose of this exercise is to correct technical mistakes in grammar, punctuation and spelling in children's writing was to improve their powers of expression. The discussions further indicated certain reluctance on the part of the participants to commit themselves to the process of writing, conferencing, editing and redrafting. There was considerable evidence that teachers continue the practice of inserting written corrections in children's work, and, although these may take the form of symbols indicating changes that children may need to interpret themselves in order to make necessary changes, it would be seen that considerable progress needs to be made before teachers are implementing the approach to writing that is advocated in the English curriculum and its guidelines.

Further more confusion was exhibited in relation to the writing, editing and redrafting process since some participants seemed to conceive it as a process that would always involve three or more drafts, whereas the number of drafts and a piece of writing might require further editing and redrafting and this would depend on both the purpose of the writing and also depends upon the audience for which it is intended.

Nevertheless, there was several evidence that the teachers are making serious efforts to engage with the approaches to writing as espoused by the curriculum. Some of the methods which was seen been introduced by the teacher in their class room teaching were as follows:

- By making use of brainstorming method for making the children to prepare them for writing;

- By making use of groups for the conferencing process;

- Making use of peer conferencing;

- By making the children to make use of different genres, such as the class newspaper, letters to local papers, and writing email;

- Encouraging the children to display their writing in the classroom and throughout the school;

- By conducting competitions for children's writing.

It's my observation in various schools that the teachers are seen to encourage the children to work in groups in order to decide on the various themes and genre of a piece of writing and plan for its final presentation, when they are making themselves available for the conferencing. This in fact, would have a crucial effect on the children's experience of seeking good knowledge on literature and on their own writing can also be stressed.

One of the most difficulty is of recurring issue that articulated in all the groups was the difficulty of motivating children to redraft their writing. One of the common most complaint which we receive is that the children find it boring and they turn off writing. This is seen particularly in the case of senior classes. This was also a source of frustration for the teachers also, this is because that when the children did redrafting of a piece of writing they are seen committing new mistakes that also appeared in the second draft. However, it is considered that if the children had the experience of editing and redrafting right from the earliest years, and if they are got used to it, then whatever, would be the subject of the writing whether it is something that is interested to them, then the purpose of the writing would be clear to them, and if they perceived conferencing as something more than the mere correcting of mistakes, then they took a more positive view of it. Children were also quite happy to draft a paragraph but at the same time showed great reluctance to draft a whole piece. There was a general agreement that the word processing would help them to motivate the children to draft, redraft and made it much more manageable than doing it by hand.

On the other hand, there was some acknowledgement that the children took more care with their writing and also produced better work; if they were aware of the purpose of the writing and its possible audience. The children were encouraged to write on a wide range of topics for different purposes and to a variety of audiences thus developing children's ability to recognize different registers of language and to write in different registers of language. Thus there was a tendency, to confuse genres with the concept of language register. Here, this seems to be related back to a narrow view were participants took to the purpose of conferencing as outlined above. The term language register was not used by any participant in any of the group, but when the interlocutor in one group brought up the subject it did not evince much interest. Only a small number of participants seemed to show an appreciation of the function of different language registers. Here, one expressed the view that exposing the children to different language registers in their reading and drawing attention to them was also helpful. It was seen during a discussion about the use of text messaging these days did have a deleterious effect on the children's use of spelling, punctuation and grammar, which expressed the view that the way the languages are used in text messaging was completely appropriate to both purpose and the audience.

It has been recognized that the teaching of grammar and punctuation is important in the context of language writing. This was more evident among the teachers who were teaching senior classes, than those who were teaching the junior classes. The potential of the conferencing process in a development of the children's mastery of the conventions of grammar and punctuation did not seem much to be fully appreciated. There was a recognition that it was engaging with the children about their writing and these issues needs to be addressed, but in some cases this does not go much beyond 'correcting mistakes' in the text. There was, a clear acknowledgement about the importance of grammar and punctuation and about the importance of formal lessons in these areas. Most of the participants felt that such lessons should be linked to common errors observed by the teacher during the process of conferencing and redrafting.

The teaching of spelling the opinions of the teachers seems to be varied. Some teachers are still seen using spelling lists without any reference to the mistakes in children's writing, and some are using spelling books. Whereas, others do note the common mistakes in the children's writing and this would help them to learn, and there is a widespread use of dictionaries by the children during the process of writing. In general, there is a demand for the need for a structured approach to the teaching of spelling. However; there is no evidence that the multi-dimensional approach recommended and outlined in the teacher guidelines have being used.

The use of computers and the importance and their values in children's writing and the use of word processing for the purpose of editing and redrafting has already been noted and found to be helpful for the children. Some also opinioned about the using of email in encouraging the children to write and communicate with their peers, in the school and in other schools. Some children are seen to use a Compact Disc that would help the children in teaching of spelling. One of the other issue that has been raised by many teachers during a casual discussion of writing included the constraints they face in a large class, where they find it difficult in mediating the writing programme to weaker children, and the unsuitability of the programme to the children from the disadvantaged backgrounds.

Bilingualism: the Second Language Concept

Bilingualism is a term in which one can encounter and come across various new terms, it is very important and useful to have an understanding of these terms, otherwise this subject would become rapidly impenetrable. Here are some of the more frequently encountered terms. Of these is the term, what is bilingualism? There are different theorists will have different definitions and will also disagree on the fundamental question of just where exactly a person moves from monolingual status to that of being bilingual.

This can range from a simple understanding of two languages to the ability to produce meaningful utterances in the two languages to the mastery of the two languages. A more obvious distinction that can be made when a person is unable to make meaningful utterances in a second language but can understand utterances made by another in that language. The Linguists generally characterize this as **passive bilingualism** or **receptive bilingualism** or **semi-bilingualism**.

The degrees of bilingualism exist in the same way as degrees of proficiency exist in all aspects of human endeavor. So there are also degrees of facility in another language. This brings us to the concept of the balanced bilingual where a person's command of a second language is more or less equal to the first. Linguists use varying measurements to ascertain if an individual is a balanced bilingual, frequently using rating scales of a plus and minus nature. When the aggregate result emerges at zero, or near zero, then balanced bilingualism is established. This facility is also referred to as **equilingualism.**

Sociolinguists will talk frequently about 'additive' and 'subtractive' bilingualism, both of which is attended by subjectivity and this may have a bearing in the emerging debate that takes place. **'Additive' bilingualism** is when a society sees another language as a high- status entity, a type of academic or social enrichment for the learner. On the other hand, **'subtractive' bilingualism** is connected with the denigration of ethnic or cultural values, emanating from a decline in the status of a language and its gradual replacement by a more powerful one.

When we are speaking of the replacement of one language by another, then it is also worth mentioning that the **transient and static bilingualism**. The former characterizes a temporary stage in the use of one or other language exclusively; the latter characterizes a situation in which the language-frontier has remained stable for a long period with notable numbers of bilingual people on both sides of it. Another term that is met in this area is **diglossia** and is frequently used at interchangeably with bilingualism. Fishman (1968) distinguishes between the two:

"Bilingualism is essentially a characterization of individual linguistic versatility whereas diglossia is a characterization of the societal allocation of functions to different languages..." In other words, psychologists and psycholinguists talks about bilingualism, while sociologists and sociolinguists will use the term diglossia. All of the above draws attention to the fact that a consideration of bilingualism is not straightforward and, in talking about it, people may very well themselves bespeaking in a sort of divers' tongues and with divergent conceptualizations in mind.

Intelligence and Cognitive Functioning - Bilingualism

A lot of research has been carried out on bilingualism and intelligence but that lacked validity due to flaws within the body of research, the work was unsatisfactory due to sampling techniques and lack of control over the variables led to the results that was spurious in the conclusions that was drawn after the research. By the end of the year nineteen-fifties, it was W.R. Jones (1959) argued that, if social class was controlled, bilingualism had a neutral effect on non-verbal IQ. This principle of neutralism was accepted and persisted for a few years until the renowned research of Peal and Lambert (1962). Although this work was shown later also to be blemished, and it did mark the resolute assertion of the belief among many that bilingualism could positively affect the cognitive functioning. However, because of the extensive raft of components that was involved in the consideration of intelligence, it probably could not be said with any great certitude that the effects are positive, negative or neutral. In other words, the case still appears to be unproven.

Results in the cognitive functioning area, however, shows a greater gravity as and when it tends to give cause for more optimism amidst the proponents of bilingualism. In the use of IQ tests, the subject of the test was directed in the pursuit of one correct answer, there by exhibiting the process of 'convergent thinking'. The divergent thinking, on the other hand, was considered to be more creative, imaginative and open-ended. This involves a search for a number of fitness for a particular conundrum. There is a substantial corpus of international research that compares the abilities of monolinguals and bilinguals in divergent thinking (Anisfeld, 1964; Torrance et al, 1970; Cummins and Gullutsan, 1974; Landry, 1974; Cummins, 1975; Noble and Dalton, 1976; Cummins, 1977). A majority of the research findings would suggest and shows that bilinguals will always out-perform monolinguals in the areas of divergent thinking. Scott (1973), states the case for a two-way causal connection,

i.e. the bilingualism is both the donor and the beneficiary from the divergent thinking skills. Even if this were to be the case, it would still give cause for satisfaction and would detract little from the validity of the evidence that has a bearing on this connection. Baker (1988) succinctly weighs the case by concluding that: "There is insufficient evidence to satisfy the sceptic, but what evidence there is leads in the direction of supporting the believers in bilingualism".

Bilingualism and Motivation of the Children

Here I have to state that the human activity is shaped in by many and disparate ways, deriving from a wide panoply of desire, impetus or force. Psychologists frequently ascribe the term 'motivation' to this inner impulsion, and few factors could claim to be closer to the central or critical aspects of the whole question of bilingualism. By looking at that connection between motivation and bilingualism, the research carried out by Laing (1988) is interesting in the context of 'once-removed motivation', i.e. the motivation of parents who place their children in a bilingual milieu. This may very well have implications for the progress of the children in any system in the time to come, as well as illuminating the faltering pathways of the times past.

Laing's study for two decades of immersion bilingual education reflects on the Canadian experience that began with the St Lambert project in Quebec in 1965. Two decades later, there was an increase in the students enrolled in immersion programmes in over a thousand elementary and secondary schools. This immersion programmes started and prospered in the face of stern opposition from several influential lobbies in the Canadian educational mainstream that maintained, as McNamara's (1966) research had indicated, that the second language attainment is usually paid for at the expense of the first. But still this programmes had great success in Canada.

The main reason would seem to be that they were, almost without exception, and voluntary. It was found that most of the parents were motivated and vibrant and was very influential. Now, weighing on these parents was the knowledge that the other language in the Canadian system would provide enriched opportunities for their offspring in a country where bilingualism was a prerequisite for advancement in the government service and for career- progression in most of the major national corporations. Most of the adults were quick to admit frustration, even inner fury at their own inability to follow a basic conversation in the other national language, though they had studied it for years as a second language. They thus wanted to see that their children spend a more fructive time at language learning in school and many were, moreover, committed to a bilingual and bicultural Canada. Others were merely satisfied that their children were emerging as something special, namely bilinguals. There may be similar motivational factors behind the phenomenal growth in the last twenty years in Ireland also.

The other aspect of motivation is the bilingual sphere which seeks to establish what type of motive is the main impetus for an individual who is undertaking the study of a second or further language. Gardner and Lambert (1972) introduced the concept of instrumental and integrative motivation in an attempt to address the eternal conundrum of why some people undertake the learning of a language with great facility while others continue to founder, despite getting comparable opportunities for mastery. Notwithstanding the fact that ability and aptitude play their part, the varieties that Gardner and Lambert delineated showed a two- pronged thrust. Instrumental motivation is marked by an underlying pragmatism, such as the acquisition of a good job, promotion, or a salary-rise. It is therefore non-social and individualistic.

Integrative motivation, on the other hand, is a socially oriented impetus, which drives a person to learn another language in order to belong to a group, or be accepted or liked by that group. Gardner and Lambert believed that integrative motivation was likely to be more influential for, they contend, personal commitments and relationships are more likely to survive the sheer pragmatic endgame of instrumental motivation. If one is to accept, even to a relatively small degree, that there is validity in what they claim then one need to examine what exactly are the implications for the bilingual education system in Ireland, where neither paradigm might be in evidence. In the last analysis, primary teachers might find themselves delivering a commodity or entity that the learner is neither greatly motivated to take on, nor which has the luxury of basking in the comfort of the once-removed motivational thrust from parents either.

Evaluation

The most important factor is that; examination is always felt and considered to be a universally an obstacle for the implementation of the curriculum reforms. The language evaluation should never be limited to their achievement with respect to a particular syllabus, but it has to be reoriented for the measurement of the language proficiency.

Formative Evaluation

The formative evaluation or the continuous evaluation should contrast with ground realities and to the problems which is reported by the teachers, thus suggesting that the ongoing language evaluation could become meaningful only when the teachers and the learners both take the responsibility of their own progress, rather than performing to external benchmarks. Teachers and the learners must be able to recognize the "occurrence of learning", which is a mental growth as it is imperceptible as physical growth.

The continuous evaluation or the formative evaluation seems to work on the ground in precisely in such an unintuitive way. This malaise can be cured only through a deep understanding of the learning process, which is an individual and self-regulatory process. For this we need a very deep understanding is essential for teachers to be able to perceive and appreciate subtle changes in the children's language learning and their proficiency. This evaluation should ultimately aim at the self-evaluation, if the learner is able to exercise choice of learning and this becomes a lifelong process for the learner. A teacher who is able to understand and knows his children is their primarily a sympathetic facilitator of the learner's self-evaluation.

Now the main question is how can one evaluate a child, even the most child centered method of evaluation would be an anxiety provoking for some, there is no question that a system of evaluation should be put in place. The learner participates in the language evaluations with more comfort when the experience is not always a failure and the outcome can be seen as legitimate and the appropriate way towards the next step in learning. For most of the children, the immediate role played by current evaluation methods within the learning process is still not clear. The continuous or formative evaluation has to be facilitated and a guided teaching is needed by determining the learner's current stage of development or their attainment in order to identify the zone of proximal developmental learning attainments are the results of language opportunities.

Speaking or Beginning to speak

When the child learns in mother tongue, then the child's speech progresses from one word, mostly nouns, stage to the production of multi word sentence with verbs, auxiliaries, determiners, adjectives and prepositions. Studies carried out by CIEFL suggests that the second language learner – speech progresses through similar stages. The learners control of the language is reflected in longer means length of utterance, sustained language input is reflected in such a growth in its output. The teacher can get an intrinsic sense of language growth in the child with such a task that is administered at three to four months' intervals.

The results of such an evaluation can be –

a) In the form of an entry in a portfolio that is maintained for each child.

b) Recorded in teacher and/or in the learner diaries. The teacher diaries act as a source for teacher development and are being widely discussed. Learners can also be encouraged to maintain private, frank diaries of their learning experiences, in a language they know to monitor their own progress.

Reading- Self-Monitoring for Comprehension and Understanding the Difficulty Levels

Reading programme such as in English do have a built in assessment, with cards arranged in graded levels of difficulty for monitoring progress. They need standardization for evaluation. The child develops some sub skills in reading.

a) Reading aloud – by doing so, here the child becomes more proficient in decoding. They read faster with fewer mistakes. There may be children who could progress from the mere spelling out of the letters of a word, to spelling and sounding out of words using spelling out as a "word attack" skills for new words.

b) Scanning a text for seeking information.

c) Reading for given information.

d) Reading for inference.

e) Extended reading.

The testing of writing and learning can similarly be broken up into sub skills. This sort of testing can be complemented by integrated language tests. The sub skill approach to evaluation would reflects the teacher's intuition that a particular student may have a particular strength, extroverted, articulate speakers may not be very interested in or good at an introverted, private activity like areas where help is needed.

Summative Evaluation

Must be "proficiency" rather than "achievement" oriented, i.e., designed not to test the mastery of studied passages, but rather to evaluate the ability in the use of language appropriately in new contexts in -

• The child's ability in reading age appropriate material.

- The ability of listening to and understanding age appropriate materials.
- The child's ability in conversing on age appropriate topics.
- The child's ability in writing on age appropriate topic.
- The child's control over receptive vocabulary.
- The child's control over expensive vocabulary.

We have to develop the National bench marks for language proficiency and this can be developed, by gathering all the reliable descriptive data from the representative of all the Indian samples. Such a benchmarking of all the national norms are well known as a precursor for the adoption of support of initiatives which were also necessary in the social sciences and education. This would be able to balance the curricular freedom which would also be provided during the learning process, with the standardization of evaluation for which a certification is ultimately requires.

The benchmarking should always lead to a set of Natural English Language Tests, this is a bank of tests that the learners and teachers can use it for self-evaluation by just opting to take them. These tests should allow us for a much finer measures of proficiency than a broad overall grade or score.

Standardized National Benchmarks for Language skills that culminate in a set of national English Language Tests for various levels will –

i.   Allow individual schools or students to get a sense of where they stand, their strength and weakness, and how to progress.

ii. Balance freedom of learning with standardization of assessments and

iii. Delink failure in English at class tenth and provide an alternative route for English certification outside the regular school curriculum.

Conclusion

The teaching of English language in India has not gained momentum even after seventy-five years of our independence, but the statistics of the population in India, speaking English gives an insight. However, there is a demand for learning English even in the remotest part of our country. This is because of the position what the English language has taken today as a global language. Study of English has been demanded by the public right from the lower class. But the sorriest part of the whole story is that we are not able to provide the best quality of education in the English language as required by the public.

Teaching of English in Kendriya Vidyalaya's too is not to the mark these days, though the syllabus for the English course is at a high level at par with Hindi. I am in the opinion that the type of English which was taught in the past about 35 to 40 years ago when we were the students of KV was far better and good were the teaching of grammar, drafting of articles etc. was emphasized. The English course consisted of the prose, poetry, supplementary reader, and a novel, during my times we had the Charles Dickens – A tale of two cities. The teaching of grammar was done right from the 6th class on wards. I feel that the English syllabus was quite superior than the present days communicative English. The introduction of the Communicative English has diluted the syllabus and has made the children poor in communicative skills, as a result we have to introduce the Assessment of Speaking and Listening skills (ASL) for the students of class IX to XII now. By introducing this in the syllabus has put an additional burden to the children during their examination. The teaching of grammar has become a scarce part in the English language teaching now as compared to the past.

If we have to achieve something the best result in the learning of English language among our children, then the teaching of English should be starting from class one onwards in the primary level. When the child enters the school premises for the first time, we can see them talking very good language that is spoken in their house by their parents, the language is crystal clear and without any grammatical mistakes. This language which is acquired by the child at his house and the skill developed by the child is only by hearing the parents talking. This shows that the child has the ability to grasp the language only by listening. Therefore, we should have teachers who are good in spoken English to teach in the lower classes and especially in class one. What has been seen in Kendriya

Vidyalaya's is that the teachers teaching in the lower classes speak to the children in Hindi and sometimes it has also seen that the teachers use vernacular languages to communicate with the child. We should be very specific that the teachers teaching class one and two should have good teachers who have good communicative skills.

Further, I have to state that each Kendriya Vidyalayas do have a properly equipped resource room. Which is also called as the Language resource laboratory. Each and every Language resource room is equipped with various compact discs containing the nursery rhymes and other compact discs which is needed for the development of English communicative skills; these are never used in the class room teaching. However, in the earlier days in class one the teacher is supposed to do and get all the things done verbally rather than in writing, usually writing work starts after a span of at least four months in the class one. However, it has been observed in most of the schools that the teaching the children verbally is done less and the written work starts off as soon as the child comes to school. In this case the teachers are not to be blamed because the parents start questioning the teacher that the child is not getting home work.

It has to be made mandatory that the teaching specifically in class one should begin with verbal teaching only where the child is able to listen and then repeat what they have being listening. Specifically, the nursery rhymes, stories, and many other communicative skills can be developed by using the compact discs. It has also been observed that in primary section most of the teachers are not fluent in the English language. Therefore, if we need that our children should come up with good skills in English language then we should be able to get teacher who are good in English language and they will have to communicate in the class in English only, so that the children will be able to grasp the English language in a better way; because it has been proved experimentally that the learner learns the language well only by listening rather than reading.

As a teacher we will have to understand that the main feature of learning language is for the development of literary. The child should be able to read, write, and comprehend the text and should be able to develop the skill and the ability to talk and convince the people about his needs and the problems what the child faces in the modern society. As stated earlier the teaching should start from the primary stage and this should start with oral language activity. This oral language activity has to be involved in which rhymes, rhythmic activities, language games of various types etc. the child should be exposed to collaborative learning at the lower level. The collaborative reading can be used at the upper primary level. However, these type of activities are very seldom seen in Kendriya Vidyalayas during regular teaching in the classes but these appear during the time of inspection by the inspecting team or by the Principal. The children should be also exposed to books, each class should have a library corner, the child should be at liberty to take any book and go through. The purpose is that they are exposed to books at an early age. Further the teacher teaching the class one should be able to read the story book slowly and explain them in a modulated voice so that the children are actively listening to the story or at times excite them by questioning, by doing so the child will develop interest towards the books and at a later stage the child will be tempted to read the book himself and question the teacher. The teacher may even ask the children to read the story books in the class and ask the child to tell the story to the class. At a still higher class the teacher can tell the child to read the story books and make them write the main theme of the story books they have read.

Further we should be able to encourage the children to read and make them understand the meaning of the words. The children should be free to come and ask the teacher the meaning of the word if they are not able to find it or the teacher should be able to make the children learn how to make use of the word dictionary. We are aware of the fact that leaning is a phenomenon which grows spirally, and it depends upon that the teacher how the teacher will be gradually help the children to grow. It also depends upon the teacher how they would include narrative information and include representative texts. Emphasis should also be laid down on the development of comprehensive skills starting from the basics level to higher comprehensive skills.

We should keep in mind that the development of writing skills among the children is something that the children will be able to develop only if the children are made to write through writing. The child should be encouraged and motivated to write on various topics in their own imagination. The children should be made to think and imagine certain situations in nature and then they should be encouraged to write. For instance; topic such as a scene of the railway station when the train comes to the station, your experience in visiting a public park or any water park etc. This process of writing should start right from the class three onwards. The development of child's imaginative writing skills is very essential and the children's ability of putting these on paper in their own words is still much more important. Apart from the process of writing, the children should be also encouraged for editing and redrafting of the article is also essential. This processes of writing, editing and drafting and redrafting should be done under the proper guidance of the teacher. The children should be made to write an article and get it edited after discussing the matter with the teacher or his peer group. This type of conferencing process organized by the teacher is providing the children proper suggestions also help them to and this also will encourage and motivate them and this will help the child to become an independent writer who will recognize the different patterns of language and the appropriate use as to how it could be presented and in proper way and through this process the child's mastery of the language, grammar, punctuations and spellings could be developed.

The greatest constrain what our teachers who are in the teaching of English language is the vast syllabus in front of the teachers. The teachers have to complete the syllabus with the specified time span; hence the teachers find it difficult to carry out various activities in the class room. On the other hand, in Kendriya Vidyalayas the teachers are given additional responsibility which have to be conducted. Most of the teachers complain the time factor as the main constrain in the implementation of these activities for the growth of our children. Though we have excelled in the field of education shall we be able to produce children at par with convent educated children who are well of in English language. We live in an era of hope now.

References

Abdul Kalam A.P.J. (2006) Mission of Education - cover story, The Week, vol.24 No.14, March 19;2006.

Adams, Marilyn Jager, (1990) Beginning to Read: Thinking and Learning about Print. Cambridge, MA: MIT Press.

Ames, Carole A. "Motivation: What Teachers Need to know. "Teachers College Record 91,

Amritavalli, R. (1999). Language as a Dynamic Text: essays on Language, Cognition and Communication. CIEFL, Akshara series, Hyderabad: Allied Publishers.

Amritavalli, R. and Lakshmi Rameshwar Rao, 2001, Coping with three languages in School: Focus on multilingual reading, Hindu, Educational Supplement, 13 March.

Anderson, V.E. (1956) Principles and Procedures of curriculum Improvement, The Ronald Press Company, New York.

Anisfeld, E. (1964) A Comparison of the Cognitive Functioning of Monolinguals and Bilinguals, Unpublished PhD thesis: McGill University.

Assessment for Learning 2016, 6th Feb, from www.ncca.ie/ga/ foilseachan/foilseachain - Eile/Assessment - for - learning pdf.

Assessment for Learning 6ᵗʰ Feb, 2016 cdn.cfbt.com/n/media/ cfbtcorporate/files/research/2013/r-assessment-for –learning – 2013, pdf

Baker, C. (1988) Key Issues in Bilingualism and Bilingual Education, Clevedon: Multilingual Matters.

Banchi & Bell (2008) Four levels of inquiry – based Science Education. Science and Children, 46(2), 26-29.

Bergen, D. (2002) The Role of Pretend play in Children's Cognitive Development. Early Childhood Research and Practice, 4,1-12.

Brewer, J.A (2004). Introduction to early Childhood Education: Preschool through Primary Grades. Boston, M.A: Pearson Allyn & Bacon.

Brophy, Jere. (1986) "On motivating students". Occasional Paper no. 101, East Lansing, Michigan; Institute for Research on teaching, Michigan State University, October 1986, 73 pages. ED 276 724.

Brophy,Jere.(1987) " Synthesis of Research on Strategies for Motivating Students to learn." Educational Leadership (October 1987) : 40 - 48, EJ 352 226.

Bruner, J.S. (1972) nature and Uses of immunity. American Psychologist, 27 (8), 687 – 708. https://doi.org/10.103/h0033144

Carleton Washburne (1939) Thirty-eight years Book of the National Society for the study of education, Washington, NIE, P-4.

Catron, Carl, E. Allen Jan (2007) Early Childhood Curriculum: A Creative play model (4ᵗʰ Edition) ISBN -13: 978-0131711112.

Challenge of Education - A policy perspective, - Ministry of Education, Govt. of India, New Delhi, August 1985.

Chomsky Noam (1975). Reflections on Language. New York: Pantheon books.

Class room Assessment and Benjamin S. Bloom; Theory, Research and Implementation, paper presented at the annual Meeting of the America/Educational Research Association, Montreal, Canada. Downloaded from Internet on 18/02/2018

Codaty, Jyotsna (2004) "Understanding Emotional IQ - The Mantra of Human Relationship", Pustak Mahal, New Delhi.

Condry,J., and J.Chambers. "Intrinsic Motivation and the Process of Learning". In THE HIDDEN COSTS OF REWARD, Edited by M.R.Lepper and D. Greene, 61 - 84. Hillsdale, New Jersey: Lawrence Erlbaum Associates, Inc., 1978.

Crow Stan (2002) " New methods of learning flourish in India" downloaded from site http://www.newhorizons.org/

Cummins, J. (1977) 'Cognitive Factors Associated with the Attainment of Intermediate Levels of Bilingual Skills,' Modern Language Journal, 61, 3 — 1.2

Cummins, J. (1979). Linguistic interdependence and the educational development of bilingual children. Review of Educational Research 49:pp.222-51.

Cummins, J. (1984) Bilingualism and Special Education – Issues in Assessment and Pedagogy. Multilingual Matters 6. Clevedon, Avon, UK: Multilingual Matters

Cummins, J. and Gullutsan, M. (1974) 'Some Effects of Bilingualism on Cognitive Functioning,' in S. Carey (ed.) Bilingualism, Biculturalism and Education, Edmonton: University of Alberta Press.

Draper, E.M. (1950) Curriculum Research – "Education Digest", September 1950.

Driver, R., Guesne E. & Tiberghien, A. (1985) Some feature of children's ideas and their implecations for teaching children's idea. In Science, 193 – 201.

Edward A. Krug (1956), Administering curriculum, Planning, New – York, Harper and Row publisher, P- 4.

Elley, Warwick and Francis Mangubhai (1983). The impact of reading on second language learning. Reading Research Quarterly 19, pp.53-67.

Fishman, J., Ferguson, C.A. and Das Gupta, J. (1968) Language Problems of Developing Nations, New York: Wiley.

Fraser, B.J. (1988) Science learning Environments: Assessment, effects and determinants. In Fraser, B.J. and Tobin, K.G. (Eds.). International hand book of Science Teaching (Part –I) Kluwer academic, Dodrecht, The Netherlands.

Gallahus, D.L. (1982) Understanding motor development in children. New York: John Wiley & Sons.

Gardner John ed. Assessment and Learning, New Delhi, Sage 2006.

Gardner, R.C. and Lambert, W.E. (1972) Attitudes and Motivation in Second Language Learning, Rowley, Mass: Newbury House.

Garney (1990) play and the learning Environment, SAGE Publication. https://www.sagepub.com.ch- 10(3)

Genesee, F. (1987) 'Learning Through Two Languages', in Studies of Immersion Language in the Primary School and Bilingual Education, Cambridge: Newbury House

Gunstone, F. Richard (2000) Chapter IX Constructivism and Learning Research in Science Education. Vol. 102, issue 7, Sage Journals, 1st Published Oct. 2000. https://doi.org/10,117/016146810010200709

Gupta, N.L. (1988) New educational Policy - A New era in Education –Krishna Brothers Publication, Ajmer.

H.K.Saharay, (2002) The Constitution of India – An Analytical approach, 3rd Ed., Eastern Law House, Kolkata.

Henniger, L. Michal (2008) Teaching young Children: An Introduction (4th Edition) ISBN – 13:978- 0135137468.

Heritage Margaret (2007), Formative assessment; what do Teachers Need to know Do, Phi Delata Kappan, 89(02), 140-145.

Hiess D. Elwood et.al., (1961) " Modern Science Teaching" The Macmillan Co., New York.

Inagaki K. (1992) Piagetian and post Piagetian Conceptions of developments and their implications for science education in early childhood. Early Childhood Research Quarterly, Vol.7, issue 1, March 1992, Pp 115 – 133.

J.C.Aggarwal (1991), An Introduction to world Education – Recent Educational Developments in the world, Vol. I, Arya Book Depot, New Delhi.

Jaireth S., (1996) "Drop out girls in India – A case study". Paper presented at the 9th World congress of comparative Education, 1-6 July, Sydney, Australia.

Johnson Alexander (1928) The care of the Aged Poor Families in Sciety: The Journal of Contemporary Social Services. Vol. 9, issue 1. https://doi.org/10.1177/104438942800900106

Johnson, E.J; Christie, F. James; Yawkey D. Thomas (1999) Play and early Childhood Development. Publisher Longman 1999 – Child Development – 372 pages.

K. Rama Chandra Rao, Where's the recovery of values? " India 1000 to 2000 ", T.J.S. George (Ed.), Express Publications (Madurai) Ltd.

Kalra R.M. and Singh R.R. (1987) Curriculum construction for youth development, Sterling Publishers (Pvt) Ltd, New Delhi.

Kimball Wiles, (1963) The changing curriculum of the American High School, Englewood Cliffs, Prentice Hall.

Kinniburgh H. Leah & Shaw L. Edward (2009) Using question-answer Relationships to build Reading comprehension in

Science. Jan. 2009. Science Activities Class room Projects and Curriculum ideas. 45(4): 19-28.

Krashen, Stephen D. (1985). The input Hypothesis: Issues and Implications. London, New York: Longman.

KVS, "Strengthening of Primary Education" Theme paper, The course module for the induction course of newly appointed principals in Kendriya Vidyalaya, (2003) KVS, New Delhi

Laing, D. (1988) 'Two Decades of Immersion Education in Canada', Oideas, 32,22 -35. Landry, R.G. (1974) 'A Comparison of Second-Language Learners on Divergent Thinking Tasks at Elementary School Level', Modern Language Journal, 58, 10-15.

Lawmann's (2014) Right of Children to Free and Compulsory Education Act, 2009 (Act No.35 of 2009) M/s Kamal Publishers, New Delhi 17.

Learning Indicators and Learning Outcomes at the Elementary Stage - 2014" by National Council of Educational Research and Training, New Delhi

Lepper, Mark R. (1988) "Motivational Considerations in the study of Instruction." COGNITION AND INSTRUCTIONs" 5,4 (1988): 399- 427.

Maher, Martin L., and Carol Midgley. "Enhancing Student Motivation: A School wide Approach." EDUCATIONAL PSYCHOLOGYST 26, 3 & 4 (1991): 399 - 427.

Marie Lall, (April 2005) The Challenges for India's Education System, April 2005, Chatham house, Asia Programme, ASP BP 05/03. Retrospect and Prospect – http://education.nic.in/cd50years/q/EM/AM/6MA/MOD01.html

Marilyn Brodie (2006) Promoting Science and motivating children in the 21st century; Science in Schools; Issue 2; Summer 2006. www.scienceinschool.org

Marshall, Hermine H. " Motivational Strategies of three Fifth - grade Teachers." THE ELEMENTARY SCHOOL JOURNAL 88, 2 (November 1987) : 135 - 50. EJ 362 747.

Mathew, Rama, (1997). Final Report (a Summary): CBSE – ELT Curriculum Implementation study. CIEFL, Hyderabad: Department of Evaluation.

McNamara, J. (1966) Bilingualism and Primary Education: A Study of Irish Experience, Edinburgh: University of Edinburgh Press.

Mead, G.H.(1934) Mind, self and Society from the stand point of a social Behaviorists. University of Chicago Press, Chicago.

"Methods of Teaching and Learning" Chapter 8 – Guidelines for promoting Effective Learning, produced by Center for Research on Learning and Instruction. Accessed from internet on 07/09/2006.

MHRD (2000) Sarva Shikshan Abhiyan: A Programme for Universal Elementary Education. A framework for Implementation, Govt. of India; New Delhi.

Ministry of Education (1996) Education and National Development: Report of the Education Commission 1964 – 65, Reprint in 1971 by NCERT, New Delhi.

Ministry of HRD (1993) Learning without burden: Report of the advisory committee appointed by the Ministry of Human Resource Development (MHRD), Department of Education, New Delhi.

Mullis, V.S. & Jenkins B. Lynn (1988) "trends and achievement based on the 1986 National Assessment" the Science Report card elements of Risk and Recovery". Educational Testing Service, Sept.1988 Report No. 17-S-01.

Nag- Arulmani, S. (2005) Language attainments and Learning opportunities: Pointers for a new curriculum framework. Ms. NFG – English.

Nathan S. Washton (1961) " Science Teaching in the Secondary School", Harper & Brothers, New York.

National Policy on Education – 1986, Ministry of Education, Govt. of India, New Delhi – 1986.

National Science Education Standards (NSES) (1999Z) Science an Inquiry: Science Content Standards: 9-12 ; Chapter 6, downloaded from the internet.

National Science Foundation, 2001, Report to the National Science Board on the National Science Foundation's Merit Review Process Fiscal Year – 2001. NSB – 02-21.

National Science Foundation,2002, "The 2002, user friendly Hand Book for Project Evaluation. Jan.2002. Prepared under contract REC 99-12175.

Nayar, Usha,(1991) " Universal Primary education of Rural Girls in India " NCERT, New Delhi.. Census of India 1991, series 1.

NCERT (1975) The curriculum for the Ten-year school. National Council of Education Research and training (NCERT), New Delhi.

NCERT (1988) National Curriculum for Elementary and Secondary Education – A framework (Revised version), National Council of Educational Research and Training (NCERT), new Delhi.

NCERT (2000) National curriculum framework for school education, National Council of Education Research and Training (NCERT) New Delhi.

NCERT (2005) National Curriculum Frame Work 2005, National Council of Educational Research and Training (NCERT) New Delhi.

Nilay Ranjan and Naimur Rahman : Role of Teacher in Enhancing Learning Achievement of Child & Emphasis on Teacher Skill Development, Knowledge Building and ICT; Downloaded from The Internet on 08/07/2009

Noble, G. and Dalton, G. (1976) 'Some Cognitive Implications of Bilingualism', Oideas, 16, 42-52.

P. Muthuswamy, (1986) The constitution of India, Swamy Publishers, Chennai Pandey J.N., (1992) Constitutional Law of India, Central law Agency, Allahabad.

Parten, B. Mildred (1933) Social Play among pre school children. The Journal of Abnormal and Social Psychology, 28 (2), 136 – 147. https://doi.org/10.1037/h0078939

Parthasarathi A. (2005) "Fusion to improve higher education" Editorial, The Hindu, 19th October 2005.

Pawar B.V. (2003) "Web based school Education in India: Problems, Consideration, Approaches & Important Features of Web - based learning environment". Accesses from internet in 2003.

Peal, E. and Lambert, W.E. (1962) 'The Relationship of Bilingualism to Intelligence', in Psychological Monographs, 76, 1 – 23.

Piaget Jean (1952), The Origins of intelligence in children. (M. Cook, Trans.) W.W. Norton & Co.

Piaget, (1972) Intellectual evolution from adolescence to adulthood. Human development, 15(1), 1-12. https://doi.org/10,1159/000271225

Prabhu, N.S. (1987). Second Language pedagogy. Oxford: New York: Oxford university Press.

Pranati Panda (2005) "Education for International understanding in India: Appraisal and future Perspectives"

Journal of Education for international Understanding 2005, Vol.1(Pilot Issue) pp.49 – 66.

R.C. Mohapatra (1990) Basic Needs: Universalisation of elementary Education – A myth or a Reality — Journal of Educational Planning and Administration, Vol. 4, No.3, July, Pp. – 41 – 48.

R.P.Singh – (1991), Non – formal Education and Drop outs _ Research notes/Communication, Journal of Educational Planning and administration, Vol. V; No.4, Oct. 1991, Pp. 411 – 416.

Raffini, James. "Winners without losers: Structures and strategies for increasing student motivation to learn". Boston: Allyn and Bacon, 1993, 286 Pages.

Ramadas, J. Natrajan, C., Chunawala, S. and Apte, S. (1996) Role of Experiments in School Science. Diagnosing Learning in Primary Science – Part -3. Homi Bhabha Center for Science Education, Mumbai.

Randall R.Vernellia (1999) " Select Teaching Methods and instructional Media" from Select Teaching methods and activities (Planning for Effective Legal education) Accessed from internet on 07/09/2006.

Russell, T., Watt, D. (1990) Evaporation and condensation, SPACE Project Research Report, Liverpool, V.K. Liverpool University Press, Copyright © 1993 & 2009 by American Association for the advancement of Science.

Rutherford, F.J. (1964) The role of inquiry in science teaching, Journal of research in Science Teaching, 2:80 – 84.

Rutherford, William E., (1987). Second Language Grammar: Learning and Teaching. London; New York: Longman.

Sacks M., Trundle K. and Flevarecs M.L. (2009) Using children's Literature to teach standard based science concepts in Early years. April, 2009. Early Childhood Education Journal, 36(5): 415-422.

Sara Smilansky, Leah Shefatya (1990) Facilitating play, a medium for Promoting Cognitive, Socio emotional and academic development in young children, Publisher – Psychological and Educational Publications, 1990, ISBN-0962596302,9780962596308, 270 pages.

Scott, S. (1973) The Relation of Divergent Thinking to Bilingualism: Cause or Effect? Unpublished research report: Magill University, (cited by Baker, 1988).

Shapiro,B.(1998) Reading the furniture: The semiotic interpretation of science learning environments, In fraser, B.J. and Tobin,K.G.(Eds.) International hand book of Science Teaching (Part –I) Kluwer academic, Dodrecht, The Netherlands.

Sharma C.D. (1978) "Use of Libraries – A guide to better use of libraries and their resources", Metropolitan Book Co. Pvt. Ltd. New Delhi.

Sharma Satinder (1982) "Contemporary Approach to school Library" Sawan Publication, New Delhi.

Shipley Dale (2007). Empowering Children: Play Based curriculum for lifelong Learning. 4th Edition Publisher – Thomson Nelson, Toronto, 2007.

Siddiqui M.N. and Yadav R.A. (1995) " Teaching of Science at Elementary Level Part – II", Arya Book Depot, New Delhi.

Snow, Catherine E., M. Susan Burns and Peg Griffin (eds.) (1998). Preventing Reading Difficulties in Young Children. Committee on the Prevention of Reading Difficulties in Young Children Commission on Behavioural and Social Sciences and education. National Research Council, Washington DC: national Academy Press.

Srivastava H.S. (2013) "Manual for Schools" 4th ed. S. Chand and Co. Pvt. Ltd. New Delhi. SSA Guidelines; Govt. of India, 2000.

Stipek, Deborah, "Motivation to learn: From Theory to Practice", Englewood Cliffs, New Jersey: Prentice Hall, 1988, 178 pages.

Swami Ramakrishnananda (2000) For thinkers on Education _, Sri Ramakrishna Math, Mylapore, Madras.

Swami Ranganathananda (1989) "Role and Responsibility of Teachers in Building up Modern India" Apeejay Education Society, New Delhi.

Teaching of Science – Internet accessed on 24/8/2006

Thanuja.K.(2016) Why Assessment for Learning, December 2016, Edutracks, Vol. 16 – No.4

Tooley James (2002) "Private education : what the poor can teach us" Feature article, paper presented at the Special Regional Meeting of the Mont Pelerin Society in Goa, India, January 2002. Accessed from Internet.

Torrance, E.P, et al. (1970) 'Creative Functioning of Monolingual and Bilingual Children in Singapore', in Journal of Educational Psychology, 61, 72 – 7. 5

Torres M.R. (1995) "Repetition: A major obstacle to education for all "

Trundle K, & Sacks M. (2021) Teaching and learning Science During the early years. Dec.2021, Journal of Childhood Education and Society. 2(3):217 – 219.

Vance & Boals (1989) Play and Learning Environment. SAGE Publications.   https://www.sagepub.com/sites/default/files/ upm-binaries/53567_ch_10.pdf

Vygotsky, Lev. S. (1978) Mind in society, the development of higher psychological processes.

Wasserman, M. Ira (1992) The impact of Epidemic, war, Prohibition and Media on suicide: United States, 1910 – 1920. Suicide and life Threatening Behaviour – Vol.22, issue 2/page 240-254.

Welch, W.W; L.E. Klopfer, G.S. Aikenhead, and J.T. Robinson, 1981. The role of inquiry in science Education: Analysis and Recommendations. Science Education, 65 (1) : 33 – 50.

Williams, C.Howard, et.al., (1993) " Primary school Repetition and Drop out in Nepal : A search for solutions, IEES/USAID, Katmandu,

Abbrevations

ASL - Assessment of Speaking and Listening Skills

CABE - Central Advisory Board of Education

CBSE - Central Board of Secondary Education

CCE - Continuous and Comprehensive Evaluation

CIEFL - Central Institute of English and Foreign Languages

DNA - Deoxyribose nucleic acid

DST - Department of Science and Technology

ECCE - Early Childhood Care Education

ECE - Early Childhood Education

EVS - Environmental studies

GRR - Gradual Release of Responsibility

HDI - Human Development Index

IELTS - International English Language Testing System

KVPY - Kishore Vigyan Prostsahna Yogana

KVS - Kendriya Vidyalaya Sangathan

MCQ - Multiple choice Questions

MHRD - Ministry of Human Resource Development

NAC - National Advisory Committee

NCERT- National Council for Educational Research and Training.

NCF   - National Curriculum Framework

NTSE - National Talent Search Examination

NVS   - Navodaya Vidyalaya Samitii

R&D - Research and Development

RTE   - Right to Education

SMC   - School Management Committee

TET   - Teacher Eligibility Test

TLM   - Teaching Learning Material

TOEFL- Test of English as a Foreign Language

UNDP - United Nations Development Programme